KU-583-928

Contents

Just decided to get married? Wondering where to begin and stressing already? Relax! This book will give you all the information you could possibly need and guide you through the whole wedding process from start to finish. Simply read on.

For better or worse...

Having the right attitude to your wedding is crucial. If you're worried that your grand passion will dwindle once you've committed yourselves till 'death do you part', that responsibility will drown the fun, or that things are just so perfect now any change has to be bad, think again. Yes, marriage will alter your relationship because, like everything else, relationships are always open to change. But change needn't be a bad thing – it can be a creative, positive force.

Certainly the figures bear this out. Despite the fact that there is less pressure than ever for people to marry – and stay married – marriage remains popular. Some 56 per cent of men and 53 per cent of women over the age of 16 in England and Wales are married and about 300,000 people get married every year.

Why marry anyway?

People marry for a number of reasons. For most, it is because they are in love and want to share the rest of their lives with their partner; they also feel the need to make a public commitment to each other. Others marry for religious reasons, seeing marriage as a union blessed by God, while there are those who feel the need for a certain security that they believe only marriage can give them.

Keeping it legal

To be legally married in the UK, the following requirements must be fulfilled:

- You and your partner must be at least 16 years old. (In England and Wales, if either party is under 18 written consent to the marriage must be obtained from the parents or legal guardian.)
- You must not be closely related.
- The marriage must take place in premises where marriage can be legally solemnized. These include register offices, premises that have been given a civil licence by the local authority, parish churches of the Church of England and other churches that have been registered by the register general for worship and marriage. There are exceptions for military marriages and for those who are detained or housebound.
- The ceremony must take place in the presence of a Superintendent Registrar, a Registrar or an authorized person.
- In England and Wales, the ceremony must take place between 8am and 6pm (except for Jews and the Society of Friends). In Scotland, you can marry at any time.
- Two witnesses must be present to witness the ceremony.
- You must both be free and eligible to marry.

Have the wedding you really want

Make sure, right from the start, that you have the kind of wedding you want and don't be bulldozed into having a particular kind of wedding just to suit the wishes of your mum, dad, future in-laws, even friends. Before you start planning, take a look at our five commandments for a happy day – your way:

1. State the ground rules early

Make sure your family and friends know exactly what you have planned. Clear up any disagreements early. Getting everything out in the open and stating your intentions as soon as possible will give you time to discuss thorny issues. This will minimize any disappointment, conflict or resentment later on.

2. Be willing to compromise

A willingness to work together is what marriage is all about, and this is particularly true when it comes to planning your wedding.

3. Agree a budget

When your parents are paying for the wedding, guest lists can become an issue. Make sure that you agree a budget early on. Let your parents know what you'd like, and then start to compromise.

4. Respect the views of others

Arguing over whether to have a religious or civil ceremony, a traditional or off-the-wall one is to be expected with parents and children. It's important to understand and respect your parents. They often have very different experiences and beliefs to you, and have been brought up with a completely different mind-set. But, equally, they should respect your beliefs and ideas.

5. Be true to yourself

What you plan for your wedding day says a lot about who you really are. It's a time to be true to yourself, and sometimes friends and family will see a new side to you.

Setting the date

When deciding on a date for your wedding, you'll need to think about when you and your fiancé, the best man, bridesmaids and ushers, as well as important relatives and close friends, are free to attend. You might also want your wedding date to be one of special personal significance.

Most people get married on a Saturday (or a Sunday in some religions). This is a day when schools and most offices are closed, and so fewer people have to take time off work. Friday is the second most popular day, especially if you've set your heart on a certain month and your reception venue is already booked up for all the Saturdays.

The majority of couples get married in June, July or August because, allegedly, the weather is better then. Other popular times of year are Christmas, spring (especially April), early September and Valentine's Day. Alternatively, what about a date that means something to you? The anniversary of when you first met or kissed. Your birthday. The birthday of your favourite film star. Pick a date, any date!

Once the wedding date is set, you and your fiancé should contact the vicar of the church in which you wish to be married or, if the wedding is to take place in a register office or civil venue, visit the Superintendent Registrar for your area.

The engagement

Choosing the ring

Most engagements are secured with the help of a big sparkler.
Traditionally, the man pays for the ring, and one popular guideline
(admittedly perpetrated by the diamond industry) is that it
should cost him two months' salary. It should be left to the
individual to decide whether that's net or gross!

It's best to steer clear of second-hand rings, unless they are
quality antiques or family heirlooms, and even then be careful. If
you suspect that your partner is thinking about giving you a family
heirloom, make sure that he knows your taste in jewellery and
your ring size. If you call off the engagement, the ring should be
returned. If your fiancé calls it off, you get to keep it, and it's up
to you what you do with it.

Your fiancé should always keep the receipt, just in case you
hate the ring he's chosen, turn him down or if you ever need to
make an insurance claim.

Make sure your ring is insured as soon as possible. If your
fiancé plans to pop the question abroad, he needs to make sure
the ring's covered by travel insurance, in case it drops from his
pocket en route to that tropical desert island.

Ring-buying tips

- Consider the type of wedding ring you want to wear, so you
  can be sure that your engagement ring and wedding ring will
  go together. Wedding rings are usually gold, white gold, red
  gold or platinum. The engagement ring generally looks more
  stylish if it is made from the same metal as the wedding ring.

- Have your ring size measured properly (in any jewellers). The ring should not fit too tightly as in hot weather hands swell and you won't be able to get it on or off. Equally, the ring should not be so loose that it slides around on your finger or over your knuckle too easily.
- There are thousands of styles of engagement ring to choose from, and it's worth taking your time to find the right one – after all, you will be wearing it for a lifetime and you'll want to love it just as much in the years to come. Shop around and make sure you buy from a reputable company.

WHAT'S YOUR BIRTHSTONE?

If you can't decide on the stone for your engagement ring, you could always choose one set with your birthstone or that of your fiancé.

Month of birth	Stone	Meaning
January	garnet	constancy
February	amethyst	sincerity
March	aquamarine, bloodstone	courage
April	diamond	lasting love
May	emerald	hope, success
June	pearl	health
July	ruby	contentment
August	sardonyx	married happiness
September	sapphire	wisdom
October	opal	hope
November	topaz	fidelity
December	turquoise	harmony, prosperity

Spreading the news

As an engaged couple, you'll be keen to tell your good news to as many relatives and friends as possible. Compile a list of those you want to contact and then decide how you wish to inform them, whether by a visit, letter, phone call, e-mail or at a party.

If you wish to make a formal announcement, it's traditional for the bride's parents to announce the news in the press. The usual wording is given in the following examples, but this can be altered easily to suit your personal circumstances.

For alternative wordings to suit your personal circumstances, look at: *www.confetti.co.uk/ weddingplanner/p11*

Wording for a local newspaper

Mr and Mrs Robert Smith of Spring Cottage, Dover, Kent are delighted to announce the engagement of their daughter Anne Jane to Mark, son of Mr and Mrs Brian Shaw of Kingsbridge, Devon.

Wording for a national newspaper

The engagement is announced between Mark, younger son of Mr and Mrs Brian Shaw of Kingsbridge, Devon, and Anne Jane, only daughter of Mr and Mrs Robert Smith of Dover, Kent.

Getting in first

If you're planning on marrying at a very popular time of year or in peak holiday season, it's a good idea to send out 'save the date' cards. These can be very simple and read: 'Julia and Matt are pleased to announce their engagement, and hope you will save the date of 24 July, 2004 for their wedding.'

How to celebrate

Announce your engagement to the world by setting up a personal web page. Click on: *www.confetti.co.uk/ weddingplanner/p12*

You may prefer to keep your celebrations to a romantic dinner for two or a special holiday together and leave celebrating with friends and family for the wedding itself. Or you may prefer an informal meal with both sets of parents, which is a great way of introducing them to each other. At the other extreme, you might want to celebrate with a big party!

Having a party

There's no set time as to when an engagement party should be held, but, in general, it tends to work best as an evening event. If, however, you want to make it a more informal occasion, perhaps with lots of children, there's no reason why it couldn't be held on a Saturday afternoon in your garden.

An engagement party need not be held on the day of your announcement, unless you're thinking of springing a surprise on your guests. However, it should not be planned too far in advance, otherwise it could end up too close to the actual wedding date.

How many people you invite will depend entirely on whether you want a small and intimate gathering with your family and closest friends or a big bash with all your friends. Do you want to introduce people to your partner and get as many people together as possible, or are you after something more focused?

At any engagement party, large or small, it's important to check that both sets of parents are free. For some couples, this may be the first chance for their respective parents to meet and welcome each other into their families.

The venue can simply be a get-together in the family home, in which case it's traditionally hosted by the bride's parents. Alternatively, it can be a more formal affair in a hall with caterers or a private function room in a restaurant or pub.

Send out invitations one to two months in advance. If your parents are hosting the party, then the invitations should come from them. An engagement party is not a dress rehearsal for the big day, so don't feel that you have to invite *all* your relatives *and* your parents' friends *and* business associates.

Even if you're holding the party at home, it's a good idea to hire caterers, leaving you, your family and friends free to have a good time. You may want to think about having a few bottles of champagne to open when the announcement is made. Allow at least two months to book up caterers or a restaurant – the bigger the party, the longer the notice you need to give.

If you're throwing an informal gig at home, you'll probably get away with your CD player and a couple of party CDs. For a bigger event, if you haven't got a friend to oblige with the DJing, it's worth hiring a professional DJ or even a live band or singer.

Hen & stag parties

Planning the hen and stag parties isn't your responsibility – you have enough to do in the lead-up to the wedding! – so this is really information you'll want to share with the chief bridesmaid and best man, or whoever is planning your traditional 'last night of freedom'.

Traditionally, the groom/bride is kept in the dark about his/her stag/hen do, but to make sure you enjoy your surprise, drop some hints. Whoever is organizing this will be grateful to know the sort of celebration you want. They'll also need to check with you who you want to invite. Are work colleagues and parents welcome or just close friends? Think about the group's ages and interests – different activities throughout the day may need to be organized, for example, go-karting for all, after which parents and the younger contingent can leave while the big boys and girls go clubbing.

Perfect planning

The night before the wedding is a definite no-no for the stag and hen parties. The best time is at least a week before the big day and with both parties happening at the same weekend – this means you won't lose two weekends together in the crucial last few planning weeks leading up to the wedding. You'll also need to think about the party location. Do most of your friends live in one area, or is there a central town that's easily accessible for everyone?

If help is needed organizing your hen and stag parties, click on: *www.confetti.co.uk/ weddingplanner/p15*

Paying up

The stag/hen costs should be divided among the group – you and the groom shouldn't have to pay for anything. If a pub crawl is planned, the money needs to be sorted out before people get too carried away – it's a good idea for everyone to be asked to contribute towards a kitty at the start of the evening. If it's an action day or weekend away that involves making a group booking, a note/e-mail can be sent in advance to everyone taking part asking for a cheque to cover costs. The best man or chief bridesmaid should make it clear that unless they pay up their places can't be reserved!

On the day

The main challenge now is to keep the momentum going, so pace the events. If lots of alcohol is involved, don't let everyone drink too much too soon – a meal in a restaurant as part of the celebrations or food laid on in a pub will help with this. Take a camera with you for some memorable shots, or a video camera to record all the live action! And don't forget that it's the best man's or chief bridesmaid's job to make sure people don't play jokes on you or your groom that may not seem funny in the morning, such as dyeing his hair blue or sending you off on a cross-Channel ferry!

Places to go

Spas A day or a weekend at a spa or health club is a good option – and relaxes everyone nicely before the big day! Or why not meet up with the girls at someone's house and book a home visit from an aromatherapist or beautician?

Weekends abroad With cheap flights everywhere, Paris, Brussels, Barcelona and Rome are becoming hot destinations for hens or stags. Why not time it around a local festival, exhibition or sporting event?

Activity days Tank or sports car driving, paintballing and pottery painting are all great options for a memorable hen or stag event.

Joint hen & stag parties

While still very much the non-traditional option, joint hen and stag parties do occur. They're usually best when the majority of the bride's and groom's friends already know each other. If you are planning one, make sure it's not going to cause problems for couples with children who might have difficulty getting a sitter.

HEN & STAG CHECKLIST

Don't let the logistics spoil your celebrations. To make sure everything goes according to plan, make sure the best man and chief bridesmaid have plans worth sticking to! They will need to do the following:

- Draw up list of people to invite, in consultation with the bride/groom.
- Select a town/venue that's easily accessible to everyone.
- Decide on what kind of stag/hen party would be best for the people involved, establish an itinerary and make enquiries and then some provisional bookings.
- Pre-book everything you can so you're not thwarted by not being able to get into a venue/restaurant. Confirm bookings in writing (especially accommodation) and reconfirm the day before, too.
- Let invitees know well in advance if there's anything extra they should bring along with them – such as props, funny stories about the bride/groom, old photos, a change of clothes – and be contactable to answer any queries.
- Create and send out invitations
- Make sure that everyone knows exactly where you're meeting. Give a contact number – ideally a mobile phone number – for any last-minute changes/confirmations.
- Make sure everyone knows roughly how much the do will cost – and that they'll be helping to cover the bride's/groom's costs. Let everyone know how and when payment is to be made.
- Have a fall-back meeting-place for late arrivals/people who get lost.
- Find out how everyone will get back home. Do you need to arrange transport/book taxis/send younger members of the party home earlier?

Your budget

Working out your budget

There's only one real rule when it comes to budgeting for your wedding: plan for the type of wedding you can realistically afford.

How much will it cost?

The average wedding costs somewhere in the region of £14,000. Around £1,200 of that is spent on the rings, £1,400 on the wedding outfits and essential pampering in the run-up to the big day, and £1,300 on the wedding itself. The reception costs around £3,500 and, finally, of course, there's the honeymoon and other expenses that vary from couple to couple.

Opening a wedding account

Paying for your wedding using a credit card is likely to lead to nuptial nightmares. One unfortunate couple spent so much on their cards that they were divorced before they had paid for their wedding! Instead, open a designated wedding account and start paying in a regular sum each month, preferably by standing order or direct debit. All bills can be paid from this account and it is easy to keep track of how much is being spent, as well as keeping a check on deposits paid out for the venue and so on.

Who pays for what?

Traditionally, it falls to the father of the bride to pick up the tab for the main event, with the groom paying for the church or register office fees and the all-important honeymoon. But more and more couples now choose to pay for the bulk of their wedding themselves. It's important to work out from the start who is paying for what and whether there are any financial

19

constraints. For example, is the bride's father willing to pay for the horse and carriage to the church? And how many guests can you afford to invite to the main reception?

However, some tasks that traditionally belong to the father of the bride can be undertaken by either the bridal couple or other members of the bride's family or close friends.

The best advice is to use the list below as a kick-off point and discuss who will do (and pay for) what as soon as you and your fiancé have set a date for your wedding. See also the budget planner on pages 156–7.

Traditionally, the bride's family pays for:
- engagement and wedding press announcements
- the bride's and bridesmaids' dresses (many brides now pay for their own dress)
- outfits for the mother and father of the bride
- flowers for the church and reception (the groom pays for the bouquets and buttonholes)
- photographer/videomaker
- most of the transport
- wedding stationery
- the reception and all that entails – the big expense!

Talking money

Whatever you decide to do, the golden rule is to talk through the issue of who will pay for what with everyone involved. Be sensitive to other people's feelings. Offering money isn't just about the financial practicalities of making the wedding happen, it's also a way for your family to show their love and support. So don't reject an offer lightly – it's easy to offend or hurt those making the offer. But, on the flip side, don't be afraid to ask your family what they would be happy to contribute. People often get cagey talking about money, or find it an embarrassing or difficult subject to broach. Not discussing it properly is a mistake that can lead to misunderstandings, false assumptions or plain old resentment.

Avoid misunderstandings

To help you with your wedding finances, see the interactive budget planner online at: *www.confetti.co.uk/ weddingplanner/p21*

If your parents are contributing to, or paying for, your wedding, it's also a good idea to clarify exactly how much say they will have when it comes to organizing the event – the venue, the food, the music, the cake and the order of the day. They may feel it's only fair that they should play a part in the planning, rather than just being the ones paying the bills!

Often the groom's parents are pleased to contribute financially to the occasion in some way, so that their son and future daughter-in-law can have the wedding they want. However, this is not a foregone conclusion, and you should not expect the groom's parents to share the bill or be offended if they don't offer to do so.

If the groom's parents make an offer and you are happy for them to contribute, then make a list of who's paying for what as soon as possible, to avoid any misunderstandings. One common solution is for the groom's family to provide the wedding cake and pay for any food at the evening reception. Or you may want to do a straight 50:50 split. Tread carefully, though. Ask them first what they have in mind.

Sticking to your budget

It's essential to set a limit to the amount you spend, whether it's you or your parents paying. Planning your wedding is stressful enough without arguments erupting over the costs. Allow a further ten per cent to your budget to cope with the inevitable extras.

Look at the 'For Sale' message boards for second-hand dresses, veils and more at: *www.confetti.co.uk/ weddingplanner/p22*

Shopping around

The easiest way to save money is not to pay over the odds. So shop around for your venue, dress, photographer and so on. Ask for quotations in writing and make sure you know exactly what the price agreed covers. Remember that you may need to add VAT to some prices, so always ask.

Taking out insurance

Wedding insurance is well worth considering. It will cover you for a number of eventualities, such as damage to your dress, theft of presents, cancellation of the reception (because of illness of a parent, for example) and double booking of the venue. Bear in mind, though, that wedding insurance won't cover you if you get cold feet on the big day!

WEDDING ON A SHOESTRING CHECKLIST

- Consider a weekday wedding, when venues generally charge less.
- Check if you can supply your own wine for the reception. For your toast, opt for an inexpensive sparkling wine rather than champagne, then have a pay bar for the rest of the evening. If there's no bar at your venue, you could ask all your guests to bring a bottle!
- Hire your wedding dress or, if you are handy at sewing, make your own. Alternatively, buy or hire a worn-once dress.
- Ask your mum or her friends to do the church flowers – and save on florist's costs. Seasonal flowers will be cheaper.
- Use a good photographer, but preferably one whose company is small enough not to charge VAT. Or dispense with a photographer altogether and ask your arty friends to take your photos. At the reception, put disposable cameras on each table.
- Make use of friends with posh cars like Jaguars to transport the wedding party to the church or venue.
- Invite more casual friends to an evening drink rather than the full wedding with all its catering costs.
- Ask a relative or friend with culinary talents to make the cake as their wedding gift to you.
- Forego the professional DJ and play your own CDs or tapes – buy or record your own compilations, or ask an aspiring DJ friend to do their thing.
- You may even decide to ask guests to chip in for your celebration, although for many people this is a contentious issue. Some couples get round this by having an informal reception and asking guests to bring a specific dish or contribute to a buffet.
- Leave for your honeymoon on a weekday. Consider an all-inclusive hotel package.
- Ask your guests to give you honeymoon vouchers as a present.

Church weddings

Church of England weddings

For most people, a church wedding means marrying in the picturesque church in the village where your parents live and where you probably grew up. However, marrying in a church is all about getting married in the eyes of God. If you don't believe in God, it would be respectful to think carefully about why you want a church wedding. Some vicars, but not all, don't seem to mind if you're not a regular member of their congregation and will be happy to marry you in their church.

What is a Church of England wedding?

- It is both a civil ceremony and a religious one, where you ask for your marriage to be sanctified in the presence of God. The vicar is legally registered to perform the civil ceremony as well as the religious rites.
- The service contains religious music and readings, although secular ones can be included if thought appropriate by the vicar.

Setting the date

The vicar will normally discourage weddings during Lent (the 40 days before Easter). Most couples choose to marry on a Saturday, as it is usually more convenient for them and their guests, and prefer a time between 10am and 4pm to fit in with the reception. By law, marriages can take place on any day of the week, but they must be between 8am and 6pm.

What next?

Make an appointment to visit the vicar of the church and parish in which you wish to marry and sort out your marriage licence. If the church is in your parents' or your own parish, your vicar will organize a licence for you. Otherwise, you can apply for a common licence, which requires you to be resident in your preferred parish for 15 days. You must also be able to give the vicar a good reason why he or she should agree to let you get married there. Unfortunately, aesthetic reasons don't count and, ultimately, it all depends on the vicar's personal opinion. There is also a procedure for obtaining a special licence for exceptional circumstances. The vicar will tell you what you need to do. You will be asked to fill in a form with details of your births and occupations and those of your fathers.

At your first meeting with the local vicar, you should seek his/her consent if you would like another vicar, such as a relative or friend, to officiate at the service. Normally, the two vicars will share the service, the relative/friend performing the actual marriage, the address and perhaps the blessing

As soon as the date of the wedding is fixed, the vicar may ask you to attend a few short meetings to discuss the religious implications and significance of the wedding service and marriage.

Publishing the banns

This involves the notice of your impending marriage being read out in church on three consecutive Sundays before the wedding. If you and the groom are from different parishes, the banns will be read in both. It is customary for the engaged couple to attend at least one of the services when the banns are read.

The wedding can take place any time within the next three calendar months after the banns have been read. If this doesn't happen, they will have to be read again.

Deciding on the type of service

The 1662 version of the marriage service is written in the old-fashioned English of that time, and the bride has to promise in her vows to obey her husband. The 1928 version uses more modern English, and the bride does not promise to obey. In 1980, the Alternative Service Book was introduced. This provides a modern format in which there are various options, and the bride can choose whether to promise to obey or not.

POINTS TO CONSIDER

- How many people will the church accommodate?
- Are photographs, tape recordings or videos of the ceremony allowed?
- What are the vicar's views on the use of confetti?
- What facilities are available, including flowers and church bells?
- Is there an organist and resident choir, and what type of music will be allowed? Check with both the usual organist and vicar if you wish to bring in an outside organist, choir, singer or group, and discuss it with them.
- During the signing of the register, there is an opportunity to add your own individual touch with perhaps a small group or an individual singer performing some of your favourite music. Check with the vicar that he or she is happy with your choice!
- Discuss the order of service, hymns and readings (religious or non-religious) that you would like with the vicar, as he or she has veto.
- Decide whether you wish to receive Holy Communion during the marriage ceremony.

Order of service sheets

As soon as you've agreed the service with the vicar, the order
of service sheets can be printed. The Christian names or initials
of the bride and groom, together with the name of the church
and the date of the wedding, are printed on the front of the
sheet. Inside are printed the order of service and the words of
the hymns (see also page 74).

Make sure you order more than enough for all the guests
expected at the church, plus some spares – you may want to send
some to close friends or relatives who were not able to attend.

Wedding rehearsal

A rehearsal for the wedding ceremony usually takes place a few
days before the wedding or on the evening before, depending
when the main participants are available. You need wear only
casual clothes for this.

A rehearsal is essential, especially for elaborate weddings, so
that the main participants know the procedure. The vicar takes
them through the service and shows them their positions and
where and when to move.

The joy is in the giving

Usually the bride's father gives her away. If the father is dead or,
for some reason, not available, the bride can choose anyone she
likes to accompany her down the aisle, or she may walk alone.

If the bride's parents are divorced, should it be dad who,
although not living with the family, still believes his daughter to
be the apple of his eye? Or should it be stepdad, who has been
through all the trials of adolescence and taken on the task of

parenting with responsibility and love? If you're faced with such a dilemma, you could always have both dads escorting you down the aisle, one on each side. Alternatively, if you feel that your mother has been the constant support and carer in your life, why not let her give you away?

It is a personal and individual choice, but an important one. Whatever you decide, make sure you take responsibility for your decision and let everyone know in good time what the plan is.

Guests

If you're getting married in a small church, some friends may have to be invited to the reception only. You should make this clear on the invitation. However, if it's a large church, make sure you have enough guests to fill it, otherwise there will be little atmosphere.

It's traditional for the bride's family and friends to be seated on the left-hand side of the altar and the groom's on the right-hand side. But what about mutual friends? When they are asked by the ushers whether it's the bride or groom they know, it can be embarrassing for them to choose. So why not tell the ushers in advance on which side you want them to sit? This will prevent congestion at the church door and make everyone's life much easier. If you have a very uneven ratio of guests, ask the ushers to fill up the seats equally on each side as guests arrive.

Wedding outfits

Most people opt for formal wear – a wedding is a great excuse
to get dressed up and this can really help to make it a special day.
For the wedding party at least, the choice is generally morning
suits for the men, and the bride and bridesmaids in whatever
gorgeous creations the bride chooses. There is no strict dress
code, but the general rule is to dress for the occasion.

Here comes the bride

The wedding party should arrive promptly, with the bride and
her father the last to arrive. As the guests reach the church, they
are handed service sheets by the ushers.

The bride enters the church on the right arm of her father,
or whoever is to escort her. Traditionally, she has her face
covered with a veil. The bridal procession consists of the chief
bridesmaid, bridesmaids and pages. The organist starts the
processional music as the bride enters the church, and the groom,
best man and the congregation rise. The priest stands at the altar
rail or on the chancel steps. When the bride reaches the chancel
steps, the groom stands on her right with the best man to his
right and slightly behind him.

The ceremony

Usually a hymn is sung once everyone is in their place, then
the priest states the reason for the gathering and asks if anyone
knows of any reason why the marriage should not take place.

Having received the couple's agreement to be married, the
vicar asks who is giving the bride away. The bride hands her
bouquet to the chief bridesmaid, and her father or escort places

her right hand in that of the vicar, who gives it to the groom. The bride's father then steps back into his place in the first row of the pews on the bride's side.

The marriage vows are taken first by the groom and then the bride, led by the vicar. The best man places the ring(s) on a Bible held by the vicar. He blesses the ring(s) and the groom places the ring on the bride's ring finger. The bride may also place a ring on the groom's finger. The vicar then pronounces the couple man and wife, although the full legal requirements are not met until the register has been signed. It is at this point that the bride may lift her veil, helped by the chief bridesmaid, and kiss her husband.

The bride and groom, followed by the best man, chief bridesmaid, their parents, bridesmaids, pages and any other witnesses then proceed behind the vicar to the vestry to sign the register. Even if photography is not allowed in the church, it is usually permitted during the signing of the register. The priest then hands the marriage certificate to the groom.

At a given signal, the organist will strike up a triumphant piece of music. The bride, on the left arm of her new husband, proceeds slowly down the aisle. The attendants follow in orderly pairs, followed by the best man and chief bridesmaid, then the bride's mother, escorted by the groom's father, and the groom's mother, escorted by the bride's father. They all proceed to the church door where the photographer is usually waiting.

Making your vows

Getting married in a church offers you less freedom to write your own vows than if you're tying the knot in a civil ceremony. For C of E weddings, you are required, by law, to perform a large part of the standard ceremony vows. Usually, the only part you're allowed to change is the 'obey' aspect and to opt for 'respect' rather than 'honour'. This will be at the discretion of your minister, who may help you rewrite certain parts of the vows.

To personalize the meaning of the ceremony further, most couples marrying in a church like to choose special hymns or readings, or write their own prayers.

Settling the bill

Traditionally, the groom pays for all the church expenses. He will either settle the account before the wedding day or leave it to the best man to settle. These expenses will include payment for the church, the services of the vicar, the organist, choir and bell ringers. It is quite normal for the organist and choir to double the charge if a video is used during the service! There is no charge for any visiting vicar, so it is nice to offer him a lasting present. It is also polite to invite the vicar(s) to your reception.

Roman Catholic weddings

If you or your intended are Roman Catholic, even non-practising, you will usually be allowed to marry in a Catholic church on condition that you sign up to the following basic principles:

* You choose to marry freely, without external pressure.
* You intend to remain together for the rest of your lives.
* You intend to remain faithful to each other.
* You intend to have at least one child (unless the bride is past childbearing age).

Normally the wedding will take place in the parish of the bride and/or groom. You will need the written consent of your own parish priest in order to marry in another church.

The Roman Catholic Church's strict rules on marriage mean that it is now virtually the only mainstream Christian church that does not allow the remarriage of divorcees. Exceptions are made only if a first marriage was not recognized by the Church – consult your priest for advice. Divorcees can, however, have their marriage blessed (see page 41).

What is a Catholic wedding?

The service is a religious one, which usually also covers the civil aspect of a wedding, since most priests are empowered to act as Registrars. If this is not the case, you will need either to have a Registrar present at the church or to get married in a register office beforehand. You may be married with or without a Mass (the full Catholic religious service).

Your wedding will be performed by a priest or, sometimes, by a deacon. If you have a friend who's a priest and whom you'd particularly like to perform the ceremony, it is usually possible to arrange this, even in a church where he does not usually operate. A marriage with Mass will usually last about an hour, without Mass about half an hour. In either case, you will be able to choose whether to have hymns and/or other music.

Setting the date

Weddings during the season of Lent (the weeks before Easter) are not encouraged, although nowadays they will not be refused, except for the three days before Easter Sunday. (Strictly speaking, if you get married during Lent, you may not be allowed flowers or organ music, although many priests will not insist on this.) You should try and give the church at least six months' notice of your wish to marry. You will be expected to obtain the marriage licence yourself. The publishing of the banns is a formality that the priest will take care of.

You will need to see the priest of the parish where the wedding is to take place. He will want to talk to you about the Catholic teaching on the nature and duties of marriage (see also page 33), and you will usually be asked to attend four or five meetings. You will be asked to fill in forms about yourself and your family, your baptism, confirmation and First Communion, and provide a baptism certificate (available from the church you were baptized in).

If one member of the couple is not a Catholic, you will need to obtain a dispensation for a 'mixed marriage'. Usually this is granted readily by the parish priest himself. If one of the partners is not baptized (if, for instance, they belong to a non-Christian religion, or to none), a dispensation for 'disparity of cult' will be necessary. This must be granted by the bishop and, although it's usually a straightforward matter, you will need to allow enough time for this to go through well before the date of the wedding. The priest himself will take care of the paperwork for you.

What type of service?

If the bride and groom are both practising Catholics, they may choose a Nuptial Mass, where they will both receive Holy Communion. Mixed marriages, between a Catholic and a non-Catholic, are usually performed outside of Mass, in a ceremony that includes readings and prayers but no Communion. The vows are the same, whichever version you choose, and the bride does not promise to obey.

The order of service is as follows:

- The bride is escorted to the altar, where the groom is waiting, by her father, or whoever is giving her away. This may be accompanied by organ music or a hymn.
- The priest introduces the service and says a short prayer.
- There is a reading from the Bible. This will have been chosen by the couple and is usually read by someone of their choice.
- A psalm is read or sung.
- The priest reads a Gospel reading (chosen by the couple).
- The priest gives a short homily or sermon.
- The couple exchange their religious vows. If the civil part of the marriage has not already taken place, they then exchange their civil vows.

- The priest blesses the rings and the couple place them on each other's finger, saying, 'Take this ring as a sign of my love and fidelity, in the name of the Father, and of the Son, and of the Holy Spirit.'
- Some short 'bidding prayers' are read for the bride and groom. These may be composed by the couple themselves and read by a person of their choice.
- The service continues with the celebration of the Nuptial Mass, if there is one.
- The priest reads a Nuptial Blessing over the couple.
- If there's a Mass, the couple receive Holy Communion.
- The priest gives a final blessing.
- The couple and their witnesses sign the register.
- Bride and groom process out, followed by the congregation.

Planning the service

There is some room for manoeuvre in the choice of texts. The priest will provide you with a sample of texts and possibly hymns during the preparation. The attitude to non-biblical readings varies from parish to parish. As a general rule, it is best to keep non-religious texts for a moment like the signing of the register, when they will not be seen to be 'competing' with the Bible readings. Some priests will follow the rules to the letter, however, and not allow even this.

The same is true for music, which, in principle, should all be sacred. If the parish has an organist available, you may request their services. Remember, they will expect to be paid (ask the priest how much seems reasonable). If you have friends who play other instruments, they may be allowed to play, on condition that the choice of music respects the sacred character of the occasion and place. Few Catholic churches employ professional choirs and organists; those that do may not encourage 'competition'!

It is a good idea to check the capacity of the church before sending out invitations: don't choose a small country parish for a grand society wedding! There are no restrictions on who may be present. Most parishes help non-churchgoers to follow what is happening by providing an order of service booklet. Alternatively, it may be a good idea to produce a service sheet yourselves, once you have chosen the texts and hymns. Consult the priest on what should be included. It is often a good idea to give complete texts, for instance for the readings, and for prayers such as the Lord's Prayer, where everyone will be invited to join in. Other items in the service can simply be mentioned in the order in which they occur, to help your guests follow the service. Indications on when to stand, sit or kneel are always useful.

Making your vows

As with Church of England weddings, the standard Catholic marriage ceremony more or less dictates what your vows are. However, do discuss what you would like to say with your priest – there might be room for manoeuvre.

Some practical issues

Where everyone sits is up to you. If you are having a Mass, and especially if it is at a scheduled Mass time, you may be joined by other parishioners who are not your guests. They will usually be discreet and leave the front rows for your friends and family. There is no compulsory dress code, for the couple or the guests.

Flowers can be arranged as you wish, within reason. Many couples leave some of their flowers as a sort of 'votive offering' to decorate the church after the wedding – a gesture that's always appreciated by the priest and his congregation. A photographer will be allowed and usually video cameras, although sometimes the priest may wish to impose restrictions on when and where filming can take place. Whether you will be allowed to use confetti varies from church to church, too.

It's customary to give the priest a donation for his efforts, which will have included a fair amount of paperwork. How much is down to you and what you can afford. About £50–£70 is probably reasonable; more is generous. The groom or best man, or sometimes the bride's father, will usually give the donation to the priest in an envelope after the service. It's customary to invite the priest to the reception, too.

All in all, a Catholic wedding will not hold too many surprises or strange customs, even for non-Catholics. It will be solemn enough to fit the importance of the day, without excessive formality or pomposity. But remember: for Catholics, marriage is a sacrament and a very serious commitment. If neither of you has any real religious convictions, it may be advisable to choose a different kind of ceremony for your marriage.

Unitarian weddings

Looking for greater freedom and flexibility with your religious ceremony? The ultimate broad church, Unitarianism is a historic non-conformist faith that emphasizes individual choice and deciding for yourself in spiritual matters.

Today's movement emphasizes the shared quest for meaning, rather than any specific beliefs. Members may come from a variety of religious backgrounds, their beliefs ranging from liberal Christian to religious humanist to New Age.

About 900 wedding ceremonies take place in Unitarian churches in Britain each year.

The Unitarian ceremony

Flexibility is key. The exact form and content of your ceremony are agreed between you and the local officiant – not any supervisory body. Most Unitarian ministers and lay officials are happy to supervise 'personalized ceremonies', where the aim is to 'do justice to the beliefs of a couple, rather than seeking to use set religious language which may have little meaning for those taking part'.

Unitarians are happy to perform ceremonies for couples of different faiths – for example, Christian and Jewish – and for divorcees. In fact, divorcees actually form a higher percentage of those getting married in Unitarian churches and chapels than for any other denomination or faith.

In the ceremony, references to God may be omitted in favour of other material, such as poetry, which may reflect your beliefs. Couples can choose their own readings and write their own vows – provided that the marriage wording remains. For

Unitarians, such ceremonies remain deeply 'religious' because they deal with people's personal beliefs and convictions (conventional or otherwise) about life issues.

What's the legal position?

Wedding ceremonies in Unitarian churches are legally recognized by the state, provided there is an authorized person present – often a Unitarian minister or member of the congregation – and the minimum legal contracting words are included.

Do I have to be a member?

You do not have to be a Unitarian or belong to a Unitarian congregation in order to be married in a Unitarian church, chapel or meeting house.

How much does it cost?

The fee for a Unitarian wedding varies and is usually set locally, but it is likely to be comparable to what you'd pay to have your wedding in a C of E church.

For information about other religious marriage ceremonies, click on: *www.confetti.co.uk/ weddingplanner/p40*

Blessings

While many couples today are opting for a civil wedding, a large number still decide to have a blessing – an integral part of many religious ceremonies. And it's quite easy to see why.

Blessings are wonderfully flexible. Most commonly, they are a great way to inject a religious dimension into an otherwise fairly secular occasion, but they don't have to be religious. A blessing can take the form of a self-contained ritual that you can tailor to fit your own requirements perfectly.

What does a blessing involve?

A blessing is a short ceremony that takes place after the official marriage ritual – normally a civil wedding, as a religious ceremony generally includes the blessing as a matter of course. Unlike the marriage itself, a blessing is not legally binding – it's a spiritual way of symbolizing the strength of your commitment to one another. It's like a seal on the relationship.

A blessing service usually involves a reading, hymn or song and a prayer. You could include traditional wedding music or something that has special meaning for the two of you – there's a lot of scope for making the ceremony your own. For example, you could get married in a register office and then have a non-religious blessing a few days later on the Cornish cliffs.

If you're going for a formal religious blessing, however, you must get a priest to perform it. It will normally take place in a church, though some priests are more flexible about venues.

A service of prayer and dedication after a civil ceremony largely follows the same pattern as a Church of England wedding, though with a few differences. Banns are not called, there is no entry in the church's marriage register, the husband and wife enter together and sit at the front of the church together, and rings are not exchanged.

When it comes to what to wear, it generally depends on when the service is taking place. If it is immediately after the wedding, the bride will be wearing her wedding outfit and the groom will be in morning dress or a suit. Alternatively, if the marriage takes place in a register office and smart clothes are worn, the bride may wish to change into a 'traditional' dress for the blessing service. There are no hard and fast rules, so it's up to you to create the memories that you want to have in the years to come.

Why have a blessing?

In the case of interdenominational or inter-faith couples, it's often tricky to satisfy the demands of both religions. One good compromise is for the couple to be married in one religious tradition and have a blessing in the other.

Since Catholics are not allowed to remarry in church, divorcees often opt for a blessing. Divorced Catholics usually get married in a register office and then have a blessing later in the day or a few days afterwards in church.

Couples often consider a blessing to be a way of reaffirming their commitment at the beginning of their new life together. You can have as small or large an audience as you like, or there could be just the two of you.

When do you have a blessing?

There is no time limit on when you can have a blessing. It's customary for it to take place very soon after the wedding, usually on the day itself, but some couples prefer to have their marriage blessed several days after the wedding.

If you're getting married in a church, a separate blessing ceremony is not usually performed, but that doesn't mean it's not allowed – talk to your minister about this. It's also possible to have a blessing as part of a register office wedding. If this appeals to you, have a word with your Registrar.

For couples planning a small civil ceremony, a blessing gives you the opportunity to involve more of your friends and family if there isn't room for them all at the marriage venue. Make an appointment to visit the vicar of the church and parish in which you wish to marry.

Organizing a blessing

The first thing you need to do is speak to the person you want to give the blessing. They should be a recognized official of whatever church or tradition you follow. Explain exactly what you want and discuss how best to go about it. Remember: blessings don't have to be conventionally religious – you can put your own stamp on them, even having a blessing given by a member of a Pagan order!

Civil weddings

Why have a civil wedding?

There are many reasons why you might choose to have a civil wedding: you might have no religious beliefs, it could be your second marriage or perhaps you want to get married somewhere a bit different. Whatever your reason for wanting to tie the knot, no Superintendent Registrar can refuse to marry you, unless there is a legal reason to prevent it.

What is a civil ceremony?

- It contains no religious elements or anything with religious connotations.
- It is conducted and registered by a Superintendent Registrar or Registrar.
- It must take place after 8am and before 6pm, any day of the week, subject to staffing arrangements.
- The service can last anything from 10 to 30 minutes.
- The Registrar has to receive an 'Authority' for your marriage to be able to proceed, which can be obtained only by giving a Notice of Marriage (see pages 47–8).

Where can you get married?

The classic alternatives to getting married in a church are in a register office or approved premises (licensed venues).

Register offices are local venues that are ordained specifically for performing weddings.

Approved premises must be permanently moored, have a roof, be open for public use and be approved for use for weddings by the Superintendent Registrar of the district. This means you can't have a civil wedding in your garden, in your house, on a cricket pitch or in a hot air balloon. But you can have a civil ceremony at Pinewood film studios, on Brighton Pier or in the clubhouse at Stamford Bridge, all of which have licences. Most approved premises are hotels and almost all of them will allow you to have the reception there afterwards.

Newly licensed venues usually have on-site wedding coordinators, who will guide you through every aspect of your day. In the main, however, the ceremony follows the same format as a register office wedding, except that you can make it more personal and slightly longer.

Musicwise, you mustn't choose anything with religious connotations, but anything else goes – most couples incorporate tracks that have special meaning into their ceremony, which can be performed by anyone from a string quartet or harpist to a rapper or solo singer.

Track down fabulous licensed venues at: www.confetti.co.uk/weddingplanner/p46

The more unusual options

If you think you'd like your wedding to be a little more out of the ordinary, you could look into the following:

Marrying abroad 'Wedding packages' offered by tour operators can make this an inexpensive option, although many resorts have the reputation of offering 'conveyor belt' style weddings (see pages 55–9).

Humanist This ceremony isn't legally binding but it can take place absolutely anywhere. If your heart is set on a really special venue or location that isn't licensed, you can have a low-key register office ceremony first. For this, couples usually wear everyday clothes and just have a few witnesses. You can then hold a humanist ceremony afterwards in your dream location and invite lots of guests to celebrate the marriage (see pages 51–4).

DIY ceremony More like a party and not legally binding (couples must have a register office ceremony first), a DIY ceremony allows you to create the celebration of your dreams.

The formalities

You are entitled to marry in a civil ceremony at any register office in the UK or approved premise in England or Wales. You both have to give a Notice of Marriage in person in the district in which you live, even if you both live in the same district, and pay a fee. For this, you may need to produce some or all of the following when you give your Notice of Marriage. All documents must be originals – photocopies are not acceptable.

• birth certificate
• passport
• decree absolute (if you are divorced)
• previous marriage certificate and spouse's death certificate (if you are widowed)
• any name change deed
• an item showing your current address, such as a driver's licence or utility bill
• parental, court or guardian permission (if you are aged 16 to 18)

Each party is also required to declare their nationality. This enables the Superintendent Registrar to advise you whether any further administrative procedures or legal requirements are needed to ensure the recognition of the marriage in the country of which you are a national.

A copy of the Notice will then go on display on a public noticeboard within the register office. Provided there is no legal objection, the Authority for your marriage will then be issued after 15 days, and is valid for a year from the date of your Notice. In other words, you can get married between 16 days and one calendar year from the day you give your Notice. It is your responsibility to ensure that both Notices will be valid for the date of your marriage. Visitors choosing to marry in England or Wales will need to satisfy the residential qualification of seven days and then wait a further 15 clear days before they are eligible to marry. Visitors to Northern Ireland must fulfil seven days' residency plus wait a further 21 days, while Scotland imposes no residential qualification but you must give 15 days' advance notice.

It all depends on whether you choose to marry in a register office or a licensed civil venue as to what happens next.

For register office weddings First of all, book the date with the Registrar. Although most couples choose to marry in their nearest register office, you may want to get married in a different one. Once you have your licence, make an appointment to see the Registrar of this other office.

If you decide to have readings or music in your ceremony, this is usually submitted and discussed with the Registrar prior to the service. You will need his or her approval.

For civil venue weddings First, select the licensed venue you intend to marry in and check the availability of the Registrar at your local register office. Book them both. Find out from the venue what form the ceremony can take. If you decide to have readings or music in your ceremony, this is usually submitted and discussed with the Registrar prior to the ceremony. You will need his or her approval.

Guests

Register offices and civil venues have a maximum number of guests that can be accommodated for safety reasons, and that includes babies and children. If the number of your guests exceeds this, you will need to decide who to ask to the ceremony and who to invite just to the reception (see also pages 63–4).

Wedding outfits

The bride can wear anything, from a smart outfit or full wedding dress complete with veil to fancy dress! And the groom could wear full morning suit or perhaps a lounge suit. Basically, the day is yours, so you have the option to be as formal or informal as you like.

The ceremony

All those attending the ceremony should arrive in the building no later than about five minutes beforehand; Registrars are busy people and will probably have other marriages to conduct, so a prompt start is vital. In some register offices and most civil venues, it is possible for the bride to make an entrance on someone's arm without seeing the groom beforehand. Before the ceremony begins, the Registrar will see the bride and groom to check that the information stated on the Authority is correct and to ask for the names and occupations of their natural fathers. Any fees due will also need to be paid at this stage.

Many couples who opt to marry in a licensed venue adopt traditional church etiquette, for example by having bridesmaids and a best man. You can also set up an 'aisle' at your venue, meaning you can still be 'given away' in front of all your guests. The only real rule is that nothing with religious connotations can be incorporated into the ceremony.

Once the guests are all seated, the ceremony begins. The Superintendent Registrar explains the legal basis of marriage in this country, you are both asked to make declarations that you are legally free to marry one another and, provided there is no legal impediment to your marriage, you exchange marriage vows. This can be accompanied with the exchange of rings, if you so wish. You are now legally married to each other. The bride and groom are asked to check the register carefully before signing. Two witnesses will then be asked to sign; these may be friends or relatives. The bride and groom will usually then be invited to lead their wedding party out. The Registration staff will usually depart after completing the rest of their paperwork.

Making your vows

In civil ceremonies, you have more freedom to write your own vows – you simply get the legal part of the ceremony out of the way and then, with the officiant's approval, you can add or subtract lines from the service. Many couples like to follow the standard vows, simply updating the words with language that's more contemporary.

Humanist weddings

These weddings are increasing in number each year. They are popular with people who have no religious affiliations but who want to enter into a publicly committed marital relationship. Humanists aim to draw positive moral values from life that are based on human experience, rather than God-given. They don't believe in an afterlife, but think that 'we should try to live full and happy lives... and make it easier for other people to do the same'.

What is a humanist wedding?

The British Humanist Association describes its ceremonies as 'dignified, caring, and totally personal'. It publishes a practical guide to help you organize your own wedding called 'Sharing the Future', or you can work with a trained official.

A humanist wedding can take place literally anywhere – from your front room to a mountain top. The rites performed have no legal status at all, so if you want to be legally married, then you'll need to have a civil wedding at a register office as well. However, some humanist ceremonies can now take place in certain specially licensed venues for civil marriages, incorporating a legally binding ceremony, performed by a Registrar. There are, however, some limitations: for example, no ceremonies may be held outside and only approved readings are allowed.

A humanist wedding is completely secular (that is, non-religious with no hymns, prayers or Bible readings). This can be a particular advantage for couples from different faiths. Rather than plump for one tradition at the risk of alienating the other, inter-faith couples can design a ceremony that emphasizes what they have in common.

A celebrant trained and licensed by the British Humanist Association usually conducts humanist weddings, but you can ask a friend or relative to do yours, if you prefer. The ceremony includes vows devised by the couple, reflecting their love for each other and for any children they may have and any other facet of their relationship. The ceremony can also include music, readings and any other symbolic actions the couple choose to make.

Organizing your humanist wedding

As soon as you have decided on a date and time for your wedding, the first thing you need to do is decide whether you want a friend or relation to conduct the ceremony and approach them. If you don't, contact the Humanist Association on 020 7430 0908 to find someone to act as a celebrant. For more information, go to www.humanism.org.uk.

Once you've found a celebrant, decide on a venue, ideally somewhere that's significant and personal to you as a couple. You'll also need to decide whether you want to make the marriage legal by having a civil register office wedding first.

Deciding on the type of service you'd like and what you would like to say comes next. The job of the celebrant is to help you create a ceremony that's personal to you. They will help you to explore your feelings towards one another and to express them in words. You can write the entire service yourself to reflect the important aspects of your relationship or, with help and advice from the BHA, you can adapt one of the ceremonies they suggest to you. They also have suggestions for readings and music.

The BHA estimates that the total fee, including preparation, advice, rehearsals and the ceremony, is usually less than £150.

Considerations when booking a venue

- Find out how many people the venue will accommodate. This will have a bearing on the number of guests that can be invited to the service.
- If you decide to have the ceremony in a public place, make sure you find out if you can take photographs, arrange your own flowers, throw confetti and so on.
- Ideally, the venue should be available for a rehearsal. This usually takes place a few days before the wedding or on the evening before, depending on when the main participants are available. Just wear everyday clothes to the rehearsal.

Guests

Having discovered how much room there is for guests at the venue, you (and your parents) will have to decide who to invite. It might be nice to include something on the invitation to describe what a humanist wedding entails. If you are having a reception after the ceremony, you should make it clear whether your guests are invited to both or just the reception.

Wedding outfits

Because a humanist service is such a personal event, you can wear whatever you want. However, if you are having a civil wedding before, it is customary for the bride to wear smart day clothes, rather than the full white number, although there are no set conventions. You might be influenced by whether or not you have been married before, but you don't have to be. Brides can go for a white dress and veil with the men in full morning dress, although lounge suits are more usual for men.

What happens and when

Since there are no legal formalities to adhere to, the structure of the day is entirely up to you. This will, to some extent, have been rehearsed beforehand with the wedding party, so that the main participants know the procedure, their positions and when and where to move.

The ceremony

This, again, has no set structure. At some point in the ceremony, you and the groom make promises to each other and, although they have no legal standing, the words will bind you together in love. A number of couples like to reflect on and celebrate their relationship before they make their promises. The majority of ceremonies will include readings and music, usually chosen for sentimental and personal reasons. The most important thing to remember is that the ceremony is about a public declaration of your love and commitment to each other.

Marrying abroad

The idea of getting away from all of the hassles of a home wedding and marrying abroad can be very attractive. Just imagine a sandy beach, blue skies, a warm breeze, palm trees and the sound of the sea gently lapping on the shore while you make your vows. If this conjures up a vision of romance in your mind, then getting married in an exotic location is for you. But there are plenty of other options to choose from, ranging from a 'drive-thru' wedding in Vegas to a ceremony aboard a Kenyan dhow floating on a Mombasa creek.

How will your family react?

By getting married abroad, you are bound to disappoint some members of your family and friends who cannot join you on the day, especially grandparents who might be too frail to undertake such a trip. To appease any objections, you could arrange to have a blessing service or reception when you return, but at the very least have a video made of the day, so that you can share your special moments with those unable to be with you.

Keeping it private

Be aware that many hotels in exotic destinations perform more than one ceremony each day and you could also be the main attraction for hotel guests. Ask your tour operator or hotel for details, but if you want to be certain of a private ceremony, then consider a quiet or unusual destination.

Leaving it to the professionals

The most fuss-free way to organize a wedding abroad is to
book with a reputable, bonded travel agent or tour operator
specializing in arranging such events. These companies have
dedicated wedding personnel who can answer all your queries
and arrange every possible detail for you. Decide whether you
want something exotic or more cultural, a hot or cold
destination, how far you want to travel and a budget before
choosing a destination.

Wedding packages are available in many hotels, with some
offering a free ceremony if you stay a certain number of nights;
others charge up to £1,000 or more. The service is nearly always
civil, although religious ceremonies and blessings can be arranged
in most destinations.

Packages tend to include just your basic requirements: the
service, marriage licence, certificate and legal fees, but these differ
from hotel to hotel. If you want extras, such as photographs, a
video, flowers or a cake, then expect to pay more. Remember
that any extras will generally be of a fairly basic nature compared
to what you might expect if marrying at home. Always check in
the brochure or with your tour operator for details.

Organizing a foreign wedding yourself

You can arrange your own wedding abroad but this will involve
researching the legal requirements and residency rules and
organizing all the finer details, from the ceremony to the flowers.

If you prefer to be in control then your first step will be to
contact the consulate or embassy of the country where you
intend to marry for advice. Always check with the tourist board

IS MARRYING ABROAD RIGHT FOR YOU?

Pros

- It's much cheaper than the average British wedding. Many couples buy their own tickets and the bride's dad simply pays for the wedding package – it's acceptable for guests to pay their own way.
- You can invite just a small number of people with whom you really want to celebrate.
- If you book through a travel operator, they'll do practically all of the organizing.
- If you opt for a tailor-made wedding, you can become very involved in the planning process.

Cons

- You may feel let down after the wedding and wish that you'd invited family members along.
- Some people you want to invite may not be able to afford the ticket.
- You may upset those people you haven't invited.
- You won't have as much control over the organizing as you would at home.
- If it's just the two of you, a stranger will have to act as witness.
- Even if you head for tropical climes, you can't guarantee sunny weather
- You might be stuck on honeymoon with your family!

of your chosen country that everything's fully legal and that you know exactly which documents you need to take with you to complete your dream civil ceremony.

Try to book a minimum of 12 weeks before departure to allow enough time for arrangements to be made and necessary documentation completed. There will be more administration to be completed once you arrive at your destination, which can take up to three days.

Residency requirements range from between zero and 40 days, so make sure you check these out before you go. Even with short residency periods, it is best to stay for at least a fortnight.

This will allow you enough time to make the final arrangements and to relax after the ceremony and enjoy your honeymoon.

It is wise to take out additional holiday insurance that will cover every eventuality, from the loss of your dress to a hurricane preventing your wedding from taking place.

Health issues

Hygiene, health services and risk of disease vary throughout the world. You should take health advice as early as possible and ensure that vaccinations or preventative measures, such as malaria tablets, are taken in plenty of time to be fully effective by the date of travel. Get a copy of the free Department of Health leaflet E111 from your post office, GP or specialist travel clinic.

Documentation

You and your fiancé will most certainly need to supply copies of the following before you travel, taking the originals with you to be produced before your ceremony:

- birth certificate
- ten-year passport, valid for at least six months after your return to the UK
- visa, if applicable
- affidavit/statutory declaration confirming single status, obtainable from a Commissioner of Oaths
- decree absolute (if you are divorced)
- previous marriage certificate and spouse's death certificate (if you are widowed)
- parental consent if you are under 18 (21 in some countries)

Check out full details
of 30 wedding
destinations abroad at:
www.confetti.co.uk/
weddingplanner/p59

Do not rely on travel agents or any third party to ensure that the ceremony is valid in Britain. Check it for yourself with the local British embassy or consulate for up-to-date advice. If you are not completely satisfied that your marriage will be recognized in this country, visit a register office in Britain to double check.

On your return home you do not need to register your marriage with the register office. You can use your foreign marriage certificate to change your name on your documents and with your bank, as you would if you had married in the UK. It is a good idea to obtain several copies of your marriage certificate, just in case you lose the original, as it is very difficult to get further copies at a later date.

Blessings abroad

If you are already married, be it recently or 25 years ago, many companies offer tropical blessings and renewal of vows services to celebrate your union. The only legal requirement is that you take along your original marriage certificate for authentication, although some destinations will require a photocopy of your certificate to be sent at least six weeks before you travel. Most of the services that are provided for weddings can be requested for your blessing service.

MARRYING ABROAD CHECKLIST

- Think carefully about where you want to go, how long you'd like to be away, what kind of climate or special features you're looking for and how much you want to spend.
- Can your travel agent make any recommendations? Have they been to your preferred destination?
- What exactly is included in the wedding package?
- Will you be travelling in-season? What will the weather be like? Are there any discounts for travelling off-season?
- Where will the ceremony take place?
- Does the hotel restrict the number of weddings that take place each day?
- Is the legal side properly covered?
- What happens if it rains? Can the date of your wedding be changed, or is there an indoor venue?
- Can the airline guarantee you'll be sitting together on the plane?
- How much luggage are you allowed to take?
- Do you have the required travel visas?

- Are your passports up to date?
- Do you need to have any vaccinations? Should you start a course of malaria tablets?
- Do you have an adequate supply of regular medication?
- Have you allowed for extra travel costs: getting to the airport, extra port or departure tax, charges for travellers' cheques, passport renewal, extra cash for gratuities?
- How far in advance will you need to make the booking?
- What is the policy on cancellation/ postponement?
- How much is the deposit to secure the booking and when is it due?
- When is the balance due?
- Is VAT included in the final price?
- Confirm dates, times and details with a written itinerary.
- If you're arranging the wedding yourself, does the hotel have an e-mail address, which will make communication easier through different time zones and also avoid expensive telephone bills?

- Enquire at the country's consulate or tourist office about: residency requirements, necessary documentation such as proof of divorce or death of previous spouse, medical tests/vaccinations, witnesses and requirements for religious/civil ceremonies. Do documents have to be translated or notarized? How long will it take to process any paperwork?
- Does the venue have an in-house wedding coordinator?
- Can you arrange for safe transport of your wedding dress?
- Are discounts offered if you are booking blocks of hotel rooms for guests travelling with you?
- Are you able to meet your officiant before the ceremony?
- Will the ceremony be in English? Can you write your own vows?

- Are you able to have your ceremony and reception at the same venue?
- Will the venue be decorated? How?
- How many guests can attend the ceremony? The reception? Are children allowed?
- What reception packages are available? Are the menus flexible? Can they provide music/entertainment?
- Will the marriage certificate be given to you on the day of the ceremony or will it be sent to you later?
- Can you take out extra wedding insurance on top of your standard travel/honeymoon insurance?
- If you want to bring your own cake, check that it will be allowed into the country and that it will survive the travelling.
- Arrange for someone to look after your home while you're away.

Guests, stationery & gifts

The guest list

Deciding on the guest list is usually when the wedding party comes to blows! While invitations are traditionally sent out by the hosts (usually the bride's parents), the bride and groom should have the chance to invite a similar number of guests. One way to do it is to split the list into three – one third for the bride's family, one third for the groom's family and one third for the couple's friends.

Who to invite

Start by asking everyone involved to make a rough list of guests, then start pruning. Ultimately, whoever is paying for the wedding should have the final say on numbers, but really the hosts and couple should have the final say on who gets on the list!

You should add the names of the minister and his or her partner to your list as a matter of courtesy, and when it comes to working out numbers, make sure you include all members of the wedding party – people sometimes forget to add themselves!

If you have relatives who you know won't be able to make it on the day, you obviously don't need to include them on your guest list, but make sure you send them an invitation. Many people, in particular elderly relatives, really appreciate this gesture – it shows that you haven't just forgotten or ignored them.

Keeping numbers down

You can keep track of whom you've invited, who's accepted and any special things you need to note at: *www.confetti.co.uk/ weddingplanner/p64*

If your wedding venue is too small to invite all the people you'd like to, ask them to celebrate with you after the marriage at the reception. No one should take offence at this arrangement. It's not a cheap solution, though, and the major factor for limiting numbers may well be cost rather than space.

If money is more of an issue than space, you can limit the number of guests you invite to the wedding breakfast to close family and friends, and then ask everyone else to join you in the evening celebrations, if that is an option.

Not inviting children will also help to reduce numbers, but make sure that you inform all the parents well in advance to give them time to get used to the idea and to organize childcare (see also page 68).

Stationery

Your wedding stationery can be just a simple card invitation or you can push the boat out and have a complete wedding pack — it all depends on you and the style of your wedding. For more details on wedding packs, turn to page 72.

Designing the invitations

Your invitations can set the style for your wedding, whether traditional or out of the ordinary. You can find designs to suit all tastes and budgets from good stationers and local printers, or you can buy some card and create your own.

The classic wedding invitation is simply type (no graphics), ideally engraved on good quality white or cream card. The format is an upright, folded card with the wording on one side. Black or silver lettering is the most popular.

You can buy ready-printed cards and fill in the details by hand, create your own design and have a set of invitations printed off or create each invitation individually. If you choose a traditional specially printed or engraved card, the guest's name is handwritten at the top left-hand side of the card.

The wording

Of course, it is entirely up to you and your fiancé how to word your invitations. After all, it is your wedding day, and if you want the invitations to have only your names on them, so be it.

Traditionally, the wording of an invitation can vary according to taste and circumstances but, whatever the format, it usually states the following:

If you'd like some help wording your invitations, click on: www.confetti.co.uk/ weddingplanner/p65

- names of the bride's parents or other hosts
- first name of the bride
- first name and surname of the bridegroom and his title (Mr/Lieutenant/Sir, etc.)
- where the ceremony is taking place
- date, month and year of the wedding ceremony
- time of the ceremony
- location of the wedding reception
- address to which guests should reply

The traditional approach

If you want to follow the traditional invitation style, there are several basic rules to follow:

- Invitations always go out from the person(s) hosting the wedding.
- Invitations are generally written in the third person, such as Mr & Mrs Jones, rather than 'we'.
- When you're listing the time, date and venue on your invitation, the time and date should be written first, the venue last.
- Use titles, for example Mrs, Dr, Sir, etc., when appropriate. There is no need for a full stop after Mr, Mrs or Dr.
- 'The honour of your presence' or 'the pleasure of your company' is the normal choice of wording. The former is often used for invitations to religious ceremonies, such as a church wedding, while the latter is preferred for invitations to an event in a non-religious location.
- The bride's name should appear before the groom's.

How you break up the lines on the invitation is up to you. Generally speaking, however, names, times and places are placed on separate lines. Bear in mind that fairly equal line lengths usually look better on the page than an array of different ones.

Invitations always go out from whoever is hosting the wedding, which is normally the bride's parents. The traditional wording for such invitations is:

Mr and Mrs Michael Bartlett
request the pleasure of your company
(or: request the honour of your presence)
at the marriage of their daughter
Jane
to Mr Andrew Pateman
at St Mary's Church, Glenfield
on (date, month, year)
at (time)
and afterwards at (reception location)
RSVP (hosts' address)

The above wording is easily adapted to accommodate a change of circumstances due to death, divorce and remarriage on the bride's side. For example:

If the bride's father is widowed:
Mr James Jones requests the pleasure…

If the bride's parents are divorced:
Mr James Jones and Mrs Pamela Jones request the pleasure…

If the bride's parents are divorced and her mother remarried:
Mr James Jones and Mrs Pamela Matthews request the pleasure...

If you're hosting your own wedding, the usual wording is:
Ms Mary Alice Jones and Mr Carl David Spencer request the pleasure of your company at their marriage, etc.

Inviting children

On the invitations, make it quite clear to parents that their children are invited by including their names and let them know up front if you have made special arrangements for them, such as:'We have arranged child-minding facilities for the duration of the service and/or reception.'

There are two ways of letting people know that children are not invited. The first is to tell parents tactfully before the invitations go out. Enlist your parents and close friends to help spread the word, and have an explanation at hand. If you are blushing at the thought of having to broach the subject in person, do it in writing. However, printing 'no children' on the invitations is not an option.

The second way is to enclose a short note to parents, tactfully saying something like: 'We are sorry that we are unable to invite babies and children to the wedding.' Not only does this make the situation clear, but it also implies that your decision was due to circumstances beyond your control.

Reception only

If you are sending out invitations for the wedding reception or evening reception only, these can take the same form as any usual party invitation.

Family and close friends are normally addressed informally as, say, Alan and Anne; otherwise guests are given their usual prefixes such as Mr and Mrs, Captain and Mrs, etc.

Invitations to a blessing

Invitations to a blessing take a slightly different form because you are already married once the blessing ceremony is conducted. You may prefer to write the invitations to friends and family as coming from yourselves. For example:

Mrs Stephanie Smith and Mr John Mark Smith
request the honour of your presence at the blessing of their
marriage on Saturday 10th June, etc.

Ordering & sending invitations

You can order your full set of wedding stationery from Confetti. Click on: *www.confetti.co.uk/ weddingplanner/p69*

Ideally, you should order the invitations at least three months before the wedding and as soon as you have an idea of numbers.

Allow one invitation per family, including a courtesy one for the groom's parents and the minister and his wife. Also include family and friends whom you may already know cannot come, but who would appreciate receiving an invitation.

Don't forget to order a spare 20 or so invitations to allow for mistakes when writing them and for any extra guests you may decide to ask at a later date.

The invitations should be sent out at least six weeks before the wedding to give you as much time for organizing as possible. Between 10 and 12 weeks before the wedding is average.

ADDITIONAL INFORMATION

It's a good idea to include on your invitations other relevant
information, for example:
- any dress requirements, such as black tie or smart dress
- whether food will be served (if it's not a dinner/lunch party)
- when the reception will finish
- whether drinks are free for the entire reception

You will need to record responses as they arrive and perhaps
send out further invitations to people on the reserve list, if
numbers permit. Don't leave this too late; some people find being
an obvious second choice offensive!

Enclosures

You might want to enclose a response card when you send out
your invitations, as well as a map and directions to the ceremony
and reception venues, with parking areas clearly marked. If
appropriate, you might want to include a list of nearby hotel/
guest houses with their prices.

Response cards Many people word their invitations to include
an address to which guests can reply, but the best way of ensuring
a quick reply is to send a response card with the invitation, which
can be completed and posted back to you. If you've got the spare
cash, you could also include a stamped, self-addressed envelope –
and then no one would have an excuse for not replying promptly!

All your friends and family need to do with a response card is
delete the appropriate word or words. For example: I/We would
love to attend/will be unable to attend the wedding of (bride and

groom) on…. You could also include on the card options for: selecting a vegetarian option, writing in the total number of family members who will be attending and stating whether the guest will be attending both the service and the party/reception afterwards. But keep an eye on the number of words. This is an expensive option and printers will charge more for words over a certain number.

As an alternative, you could buy a set of ready-printed RSVP cards – something plain and simple that won't clash with your invitation design – or buy plain card and write them yourself.

It's also a good idea to add a date by when you would like to receive the replies. You need to give yourself the maximum amount of time to ask other people if you find you've got the space. A sensible date is one or two months before the event, or whatever makes sense for your arrangements. After this date, start ringing round any stragglers for their answers.

Map & directions The more detailed and carefully written the directions, the fewer phone calls you'll get from people who've got lost! The map can be drawn by hand or photocopied. Alternatively, go to a local map web site and print out the relevant page(s), or include the web site address for those with Internet access. You may also like to include details of the nearest train, tube or bus stations, as well as the numbers of local cab firms. If you have cash galore, you can have your maps printed, too, so that the card matches your invitation and response card!

Create your own wedding web page so that guests can get hold of details ahead of time at: *www.confetti.co.uk/ weddingplanner/p71*

Local accommodation For those travelling some distance, you can include a list of local hostels, B&Bs and hotels. This could be just names and telephone numbers, or you could include brief descriptions so that guests know what they're letting themselves in for. You could also give relevant web site addresses with details of the accommodation on your list. Many hotels will allow block reservations of rooms, as long as they are confirmed by a certain date. This usually allows you to negotiate a more favourable rate, especially during the off-peak season.

Wedding packs

These days increasing numbers of people travel from overseas to join in the wedding celebrations of friends and family. If you have friends coming over from America, for instance, you're asking them to plan their vacation time around your wedding, as well as expecting them to make a considerable financial outlay. By sending them a guest information pack, which includes details of travel, accommodation, restaurants and tourist information, you can help ensure that their trip runs smoothly and is as rewarding as possible.

Send guests travel information well in advance, especially if they have to book plane or train tickets. Suggestions of the nearest airport or cheapest way to obtain tickets are very welcome. The numbers of local taxi firms may also prove invaluable. Remember, out of town guests may not have a car available to them. It is a nice thought to arrange for a coach or minibus to pick them up from the hotel and take them to the ceremony venue, and then on to the reception.

Guests who've travelled a fair distance only to be faced with trying to find somewhere good to eat at the end of a long and tiring day will truly appreciate a list of addresses and numbers of local restaurants where they can revive themselves!

If circumstances change

Hopefully you won't have to postpone or cancel your wedding, but if you do, you need to let your guests know formally. The usual wording for postponement and cancellation is given below.

For postponement Owing to the recent illness of Mrs Jones, the wedding of her daughter Susan to Mr Neil Wood at St Mary's Church at 2pm on Saturday 5th April, 2003 has been postponed to 3pm on Saturday 12th August, 2003.

For cancellations Owing to the sudden death of Mr Jones, the wedding of his daughter Susan to Mr Neil Wood will not now take place at St Mary's Church at 2pm on Saturday 5th April, 2003. The marriage will take place privately at a date to be decided.

Other stationery

You may wish to have additional personalized stationery, such as order of service sheets, menus, place cards and napkins. Make sure that you finalize all the relevant details before placing a firm order, to avoid any unnecessary expense. It may be worth making a bulk order and negotiating a discount.

If you're having a church wedding, the sample template below should help you to set out your order of service. Make sure that you check the content with whoever is conducting your service before having these printed.

Front page
Church and Location
The Marriage of Bride and Groom
Date and Time

Inside
Entrance music (processional) for bride
Introduction
Hymn (include words)
The Marriage
Prayers (optional)
Reading (optional)
Blessing (optional)
Hymn (include words)
Reading/Blessing (optional)
Hymn (optional – include words)
Signing of the register
Exit music (recessional)

Wedding gift list

Traditionally, this isn't included with the invitation; guests who wish to buy the bride and groom a present ask the bride's parents for details about the gift list. However, nowadays it's more acceptable to include the gift list with the invitation so all the relevant information gets sent out together and the bride's family doesn't have to fork out for and organize multiple mailings!

Compiling your list

Gift lists are one of the fun parts of planning a wedding – after all, there's no better way to take a break from devising the seating plan than to compile a list of pressies for yourself. They're practical, too – an excellent way of making sure you get the presents you really want and need.

Set up a gift list with Confetti where guests can buy online, by phone or by mail order. Go to: *www.confetti.co.uk/ weddingplanner/p75*

Most guests welcome advice on what to buy, so make your list as comprehensive as possible to cover a price range that will suit all pockets.

When drawing up the list, be specific about what make, model and colour of item you want. Try to list many more items than you have guests, so that no one is left having to buy the Mickey Mouse salt cellar. Make sure you state how many of each item you want: matching towels don't match if you have only one!

The gifts you choose to have on your list will depend on what stage you are at in your life:

For first-timers A young couple setting up home together for the first time will want all the basics: china, pots and pans, bed linen and glassware, even the humble lemon squeezer.

For late starters Couples getting married a little later in life may already own a property or be living together, and are likely to have most of the staple household items. In this situation, couples often ask for more luxurious items they couldn't afford themselves, like garden furniture, leather photo albums and state-of-the-art kitchen equipment. Of course, it's unlikely that you have hundreds of wealthy friends and relations, but you could suggest they club together to buy an expensive gift between them.

POINTS TO CONSIDER

- Include a variety of gifts that will appeal to all tastes and pockets, so that no one feels pressured into buying something they don't like or can't afford.
- Don't just think of the here and now – think ahead. You may not be interested in a fancy cutlery set at the moment but in later years one could come in useful.
- If you want to have your wedding list at a large department store, make sure you find out when you can register, as some stores restrict registration to certain times.
- Although strict wedding etiquette demands that the gift list is not sent with the invitations, in practice many couples do so or at least refer to it – it's easier for everyone concerned.
- Keep a record of all the people who give you presents, so that you're prepared when it comes to writing your thank you letters.

Not for the first time If you are getting married for the second or third time, you are even more likely to have amassed all the necessary household possessions. So, if you are both passionate about something, say entertaining friends, you could give your gift list a cooking theme, and ask for specialist kitchen implements and unusual cooking ingredients. Alternatively, you could ask for specific bottles of wine, champagne, even brandy and port to help you establish a really good wine cellar.

Gifts for the wedding party

Remember that you're not the only ones to receive gifts. It's traditional for the mothers, best man (sometimes the ushers), bridesmaids, flower girl, pageboy and any helpers to be given presents as well. The groom usually gives them during his speech at the reception. It's also up to him to give a general thanks to all the guests for your wedding gifts. You may also want to exchange gifts with your fiancé, which you can do either the day before the wedding or during the reception.

The key to buying a good gift for the wedding party is to choose something that will remind them of your wedding day. Jewellery is always a good idea, for example cufflinks for the best man and ushers, and a necklace for each of the bridesmaids. If you give these on the morning of the wedding, then they can be worn throughout the day. For a memorable gift for the adult members of the party after the wedding, what about champagne and oysters delivered to the door? Or perhaps a polo lesson, a hot air balloon ride or a day at a spa?

To buy the gifts described and many others, visit:
www.confetti.co.uk/ weddingplanner/p77

77

Dressing the part

The bride

From ancient times, the bride has been celebrated, in poetry and prose, as everything good, pure and beautiful. That's some image to live up to! In reality, being a bride can be a very stressful experience. However natty your fiancé looks in his waistcoat and tails, you know all eyes will be on you as you walk up the aisle.

Choosing your dress

Although you've probably got lots of ideas and may well have been dreaming of the perfect dress for months, even years, it's best to seek out some professional advice. This will ensure that the final creation fits and flatters you perfectly, accentuating your good points and minimizing the rest.

A formal long dress is equally suitable for a church or civil ceremony, although many brides prefer to wear a smart dress or a suit for a register office wedding. If you're having a religious ceremony, bear in mind that some religions frown on sleeveless or very low-cut outfits.

Whatever style you decide on, it's worth remembering that the back view is as important as the front – for most ceremonies, the guests will be behind you. It's a good idea to choose fabric resistant to crushing and creasing. If you want to have a train, it's wise to make it detachable so that it can be removed (or hooked up) for dancing at the reception.

Discuss your ideas with the groom to ensure that the colour and style are coordinated with him and all the attendants. There is no need to reveal the finer details of the dress, as traditionally these should not be known by the groom until he sees his bride walking up the aisle towards him.

Be inspired by hundreds of the latest styles in dresses from top designers at: *www.confetti.co.uk/weddingplanner/p80*

Take a good look at yourself

When you imagine your perfect wedding day, do you see a realistic image of yourself? We all want to look our most gorgeous for the big day – glowing, beautiful and with the body of a Hollywood starlet, after months of dieting and rigorous exercise. But when the daydream fades, we know that most of us don't look much like the celebrity icons of glossy magazines. Worried? Don't be. Beauty comes in all different shapes and sizes, and the way to look your best is not to conjure up a picture of someone you're not – but to concentrate on the real image of yourself.

Think about what you normally wear, your favourite colours, where the ceremony's taking place and the tone you're aiming for – traditional, avant-garde or relaxed. Once you have a clear idea of these elements, you can start applying them to your outfit.

Think colour

A white dress isn't obligatory. If white doesn't suit your complexion or tastes, don't wear it. Wedding gowns in cream, pale gold, pale blue and pink are all quite usual now, and there's been a recent move to much deeper colours in shades of green or even burgundy – particularly stunning for a winter wedding.

If you decide against white, you shouldn't feel obliged to plump for a 'trendy' colour either. Far better to go for a dress in your favourite shade or one that makes your skin glow. Remember, though, that if you're going for a very bright colour, you should keep the detail on your dress to a minimum.

The right style for your shape

Choosing a style that suits your shape will make a huge difference to how you look, and it will also boost your confidence no end. If your body or choice of ceremony isn't right for a white puffy dress, don't even think about trying one on. Not only will it depress you, but you might also still buy it because of that traditional image you have in your head – and then you'll end up feeling awful on your big day.

If your shape tends to the tall and thin... you could choose a ballgown with a strapless, fitted bodice. However, if you feel that your shoulders are rather bony or that your collarbone protrudes too much, go for a long fitted dress, perhaps with a high neckline. You may feel that you are too thin for this style, but your height and leanness could be set off with some delicate detailed embroidery or beading.

To see illustrations of the dress shapes described, check out: www.confetti.co.uk/weddingplanner/p81

If you are short with a fuller, feminine figure... you could try an empire line dress. The beauty of this style is that it has a seam under the bustline and, in the right fabric, the dress will not cling to your body but flow around it. Although a knee-length dress could also look good, this longer shape will give you a taller silhouette. If you choose to have sleeves, go for long and narrow but not too tight.

If you have a very full bust... draw attention away from it by having a long bodice. Dresses that use the natural waistline, on the other hand, will draw attention to the bust area. Make sure your bodice area is very plain, and avoid low necklines. If you are really keen on detail, save it for the hem of the skirt.

If you have full or wide hips... avoid a bustle, peplum or anything tiered. Most styles of dress will look great, but make sure it's something that doesn't fit too tightly over the hip area. The 'princess' style, which is fitted on top and then flares slightly to the hem, will disguise larger hips. Even the ballgown look, in quite a simple material, will draw attention away from the hips.

If you have wide shoulders... consider narrowing your look with wide straps, or cover them completely and draw the focus to a V-neckline. It's important to show some skin around this area, but you can soften the effect by wearing a sheer wrap around your shoulders. Stay away from puffed sleeves!

If your legs are short or on the heavy side... it's a good idea to opt for a long dress. Give yourself more height with a sheath style, which is straight, but not too body-hugging.

If your arms are on the short side... three-quarter-length sleeves will help to make them look longer, but, whatever you do, do not go sleeveless.

If your arms are chubby... go for long and simple sleeves that are not skin tight.

Shopping around

Brides have a few options to choose from, which include ready-made, made-to-measure and couture dresses.

It makes good sense to start dress hunting up to 12 months before the ceremony, especially if you've set a date during the busy summer months. The final fitting should be two weeks before the wedding.

The cost of dresses varies greatly, so have a clear idea of how much you are prepared to spend before you go shopping. It is best to try on as many different styles as you can at first and view them from all angles. Take along a trusted friend for honest advice, and don't feel pressured by salespeople. Take your time to choose and enjoy the shopping spree!

POINTS TO CONSIDER

- How much is the deposit and when is it due?
- When is the balance due?
- Is VAT included in the final price?
- How far before the wedding must you order your dress?
- How many fittings will you need?
- Can you arrange at least one fitting with your bridal lingerie, shoes and other accessories?
- Confirm appointments for fittings and collection dates with a written contract.
- How far before the wedding can you expect your dress to arrive?
- What is the policy on cancellation/postponement?
- Have you insured the dress?
- If you hire your dress, check all the details before making your booking. Will your chosen dress be available on the day, cleaned and ready to collect? Does the hire cost cover the entire 24-hour period? Does the dress have to be cleaned before it is returned (this is very expensive)?

Specialist bridal shops and stores keep dozens of styles in a range of sizes and most provide a fitting and alteration service at a small extra cost. You may need to book an appointment in some of the most popular shops.

If you feel that buying a dress is too extravagant, hiring a dress or wearing a worn-once dress is a popular option, and specialist hire shops offer an extensive range to suit all pockets.

Making your own dress

If you can't find the dress of your dreams at a bridal or hire shop, you may have to get it made or make it yourself.

First, consider whether you feel confident enough to make your own dress. It may be far better to choose a pattern and material and employ a professional dressmaker. Your dressmaker should be happy to incorporate your individual preferences and finishing touches, such as lace inserts, ribbons and embroidery.

You ought to get several fittings, and some dressmakers will even visit you on your wedding day to make last-minute adjustments. All this costs money but, for peace of mind, it's normally worth every penny!

Find companies that will reinvent your wedding dress so that you can wear it after the big day. Click on: *www.confetti.co.uk/ weddingplanner/p84*

After the wedding

You may want to choose a style of dress that can be dyed or adapted for use as a black tie or cocktail dress afterwards. There are many firms that can provide such a service. If you wish to have your wedding dress dry-cleaned, do so within a few weeks of the wedding. Some firms sell special boxes to preserve your dress so that it will remain in pristine condition for years.

Choosing the accessories

Depending on the style of dress you choose, you'll also have to make decisions on a whole host of accessories.

Veils & headdresses

Wedding veils are generally made of lace or tulle and secured by a circlet of flowers or a tiara. The general rule is the more formal the dress, the longer the veil. You also need to think about how your veil will be held in place.

Veils and tiaras are often treasured in families and worn by generations of brides, so you might be able to borrow one or both from your own family or the groom's. Make sure you practise putting on your veil at least a week before the wedding, and don't leave it till the last minute on the actual day.

You could have a headdress made up with real flowers – usually the same varieties as in your bouquet – which should be made up and delivered on the day by the same florist. Most florists offering a bridal service will have several designs of headdresses from which to choose.

Fabric flowers may prove less of a worry, as obviously they will remain in perfect condition throughout the day. Bridal shops and stores have a wide range to choose from. Try on a selection of headdresses before buying one, preferably with your dress on.

You may prefer to wear a hat to complete your outfit, particularly if your dress is not a traditional wedding dress.

Lingerie

When it comes to lingerie, you will need to try everything on with your dress in order to check that there are no lines showing or straps peeping out! Remember that, although you want to feel glamorous on your wedding day, you want to feel like you. If you are simply not a stockings and suspenders person, don't torture yourself by wearing them on the day.

Shoes

For more accessories of all types, see the accessories database online at: www.confetti.co.uk/weddingplanner/p86

Shoes are the most important accessories. They need to be comfortable, non-slip and with a heel to complement both your height and the dress. The sooner you find your perfect pair the better! Take them with you to dress fittings. On the day, don't forget to have a spare pair of stockings or tights to hand for those inevitable ladders. Wear your shoes around the house before the wedding to wear them in – trying to look serene and beautiful is not easy when that blister on your heel is getting bigger by the minute! If you're scared of getting ivory satin shoes dirty before your wedding, put a pair of clean pop socks over them for protection.

Gloves

If you're wearing gloves, the ring finger on the left hand must be exposed for the exchange of rings. This is accomplished by simply cutting along the base where the finger joins the main body of the glove. Some gloves are available 'ready-ripped'.

Something old...

Tradition states that a bride should have 'something old, something new, something borrowed and something blue'. This apparently brings all the available mystical influences into her possession! Something old is the past, something new the future, and something borrowed the present. Something blue symbolizes purity. In addition, carrying a lucky charm, such as a silver horseshoe, is still a popular thing to do.

Your going-away outfit

A bride's going-away outfit, like her wedding dress, is often a source of great public interest. An elegant dress or suit is often chosen for town weddings. For a country wedding, the outfit can be more casual. However, you may like to consider changing out of your dress earlier at the reception so you can strut your stuff unimpeded on the dance floor! Remember that it is not obligatory to have a going-away outfit.

Pregnant brides

Well, you're not alone. One London wedding dress store recently estimated that up to 20 per cent of its customers were expecting. But none of the major stores carries specific maternity lines, leaving many brides-to-be in fear that they won't be able to find anything to flatter their burgeoning figures. Although they may not overly advertise the fact, wedding dress suppliers do stress that they will try to ensure that the pregnant bride won't miss out on the dress of her dreams.

What to wear?

Bump doesn't have to equal frump, but any pregnant bride has to take certain things into account. The big day is a long day, and, if you are expecting or have just had a baby, you're bound to get tired more easily than usual. That means that comfort has to be paramount when choosing what to wear. Don't try to force yourself into a corset – you'll faint. And be honest with the person who is providing the dress. Tell them that you're pregnant – even if you don't want anyone else to know.

Your dress will have to accommodate your changing shape, so look for a dress supplier who will carry out alterations as close to the wedding day as possible.

If you want to try and disguise the fact that you're pregnant, going one size up and getting the top part of the dress altered is an option, and a big bouquet will help, too.

Of course, style need not be sacrificed for the sake of comfort, but for most pregnant women tight waists, figure-hugging dresses and tightly laced bodices will be out. Instead, why not show off your new curves with a focus on the shoulders and bust?

Perfect for pregnant brides are empire line, princess line or A-line dresses. In all these styles, the dress flares from under the bust, although the empire line has a straighter skirt. You could add a chiffon overdress to complete the outfit. Alternatively, you could plump for a medieval-style dress with long, flowing sleeves.

The bridesmaids

It's usual for the bride to choose the bridesmaids' outfits. Traditionally, these are paid for by the bridesmaids themselves for the privilege of taking part. Nowadays, payment is either shared or negotiated – but discuss this up front. Once you add up the cost of the material, shoes, dressmaking and accessories, it can be an expensive business!

Choosing their dresses

The bride's choice of bridesmaids' dresses will depend on several factors, most importantly what she is wearing herself. If she chooses a long elaborate gown, then her bridesmaids can be similarly attired. If, however, she decides to marry in a shorter, simpler style, then it would look odd for the attendants to be dressed in frills and flounces.

If the bridesmaids are of varying shapes and sizes, you have the complicated task of choosing a style and colour to suit them all. One solution is for you to choose material of a certain shade and for the bridesmaids to have dresses made in that same shade and in a style that suits them. Once the style and fabric have been chosen, your chief bridesmaid should coordinate the other bridesmaids' fitting sessions, to take the pressure off you.

If lots of money is being spent, it's wise to get something that can be worn again, to a ball or a smart dinner, or you may want to sell the dresses after the wedding.

Making the bridesmaids' dresses is a much more popular option than making your own dress because they are often simpler in design and decoration, and they can be made at home more easily.

Accessories

Bridesmaids often wear headdresses and usually carry flowers.
Colour and style are important here, as a certain style of
headdress may not suit all age groups and individual colourings.

Shoes are generally formal, matching coloured or light court
shoes or sandals for the adults, with soft shoes, such as ballet
pumps, for the young ones.

Bridesmaids carry bouquets, posies or flower baskets. Again,
the colours of the chosen flowers should enhance the bride's
chosen colour scheme.

Flower girls & pageboys

The job of these junior helpers is chiefly to take part in the
bridal procession to and from the marriage venue, looking as
sweet and endearing as possible.

Flower girls generally wear a mini version of either the bride's
dress or the bridesmaids' dresses. Usually, they carry a posy
or a basket of flowers or petals, which they strew up the aisle in
front of the bride. However, some ministers don't appreciate this,
so get permission first!

Pageboys are often dressed in sailor suits, or Little Lord
Fauntleroy outfits. Usually, you can get only a very young boy to
agree to this kind of outfit without a fight! Alternatives are to
dress the pageboys in smart trousers and waistcoats, or even in
a slightly less overwhelming kind of morning dress (if that's what
the ushers are wearing). They do not carry flowers.

CHECKLIST FOR THE MEN

If you'd like to be sure that your sartorial influence extends to the groom and the men of the wedding party, make sure that you pass on the following information.

- If this year's look is just a little bit too flamboyant, take comfort in tradition. Opt for a classic morning suit or black frock coat, which can be jazzed up with a cravat in the season's colours.
- Always choose a suit because it looks good on you, and not because it's a designer label.
- When choosing a waistcoat, make sure it fits well – you'll want to present a neat silhouette when you take off your jacket.
- If you're getting hitched on the beach, keep your cool by wearing a white cotton shirt with the top button undone, a plain waistcoat and linen/cotton mix trousers.
- Make sure you know what colour scheme your bride has decided on, to ensure that there are no nasty colour clashes.

- Well-polished, black leather lace-ups such as Oxfords look good with most suits, but for a casual beach wedding, opt for sandals or smart leather flip-flops. Whatever your choice, wear them in around the house for a couple of days. This will keep you blister-free on the big day.
- If you're planning on wearing a kilt, make sure this doesn't come as a complete surprise to the bride!
- If you want the best man, ushers and fathers to dress in the same style as the groom, make sure they consult early. Outfits may need to be hired, especially if you choose something few people have in their wardrobes, such as morning suits (and top hats).

Health & beauty

Getting into shape

You may have decided to lose a few pounds before your wedding day, but don't set yourself unrealistic targets. It's never easy to stick to a diet, and when you're feeling stressed, it's even harder.

Effective dieting isn't about calorie counting, it's about changing your eating habits. So tuck into more high-carbohydrate foods (cereals, bread, rice, pasta, potatoes) and fewer high-fat foods (cheese, ice cream, red meat, fried breakfasts). Get into the habit of eating like this all the time and aim to lose 1–2 pounds a week.

Try to take some extra exercise, such as walking to work or swimming. This should burn off a few pounds but, more importantly, it will make you feel healthier and more relaxed.

If your budget allows, you might like to treat yourself to a few days at a health spa. Expert advice, beauty therapies and exercise facilities will help you come away feeling great.

Pre-wedding nerves

It's quite common for prospective brides – and grooms – to suffer from pre-wedding nerves, but it's important to minimize that stress, otherwise you will end up making yourself ill.

At some point, you might wonder if you're doing the right thing by getting married at all. This can be a very scary feeling, especially if money has already been spent and you feel that everyone has great expectations for you and your partner.

As a rule of thumb, it's only if these misgivings last for several weeks that you need to consider seriously if you're doing the right thing. Take a deep breath and tell your partner how you feel. Consider putting the wedding date back to give you both time to resolve any issues.

How to keep your cool

- Remember that an engagement is supposed to be an exciting time spent thinking about your betrothed and imagining the wonderful future you will have together.
- Decide with your fiancé early on who's going to do what and stick to what you agree.
- Try not to let the minute details become all consuming. Instead, delegate to friends and relatives and enjoy yourself.
- Buy a wall planner and write down vital dates.
- Build some planning-free zones into your timetable, such as going out for a meal with your fiancé and agreeing not to mention the wedding.
- Don't worry about being too bossy or opinionated. Most people you deal with, such as the caterer or the photographer, will appreciate it if you know exactly what you want and tell them so. Keep pictures of flowers/table settings/hairstyles and so on that you like in a file so that you have a visual reference to show people.
- Plan a treat for yourself and your fiancé about a month after the wedding – that way you'll have something to look forward to when you come back from your honeymoon.

Planning your look

For the big day, the idea is to look like a better version of yourself rather than going for a completely new look, so learn the trick of enhancing your best features.

Get into a regular skincare routine a few months before the wedding. Invest in some good products, and cleanse, tone and moisturize every morning and evening. To find out which products suit your skin, have a makeover in a department store. You'll receive lots of help and advice, and the fee is usually redeemable against any products bought.

When it comes to make-up colour schemes, think about the shade of your dress. Pink, silver or gold hues can be echoed in your make-up for a coordinating finished look.

Using a professional make-up artist

To find make-up artists in your area, click on: www.confetti.co.uk/ weddingplanner/p95

This is a really good idea, especially if you don't usually wear make-up and need an experienced touch! Independent make-up artists will carry out a trial run a month or so before the big day, then come to your home on the morning of the wedding to recreate the look. Prices can vary substantially, so make sure you get a written quotation in advance that states exactly what is included. You could try to negotiate a cheaper discounted rate for your mum and bridesmaids to have their make-up applied professionally as well.

Choosing your hairstyle

Start thinking about your hairstyle as soon as you've set a wedding date. This will give you time to grow your hair, experiment with shorter styles or get used to subtle colouring. Don't be tempted to go for a dramatically different do for your wedding day, though – remember that even though the hairstyle won't last forever, your photos will!

Book a consultation at a couple of local salons until you find a stylist you feel comfortable with and who understands your hair type. Remember to take along as much info about your special day with you as possible – for example, a photo of your dress and a fabric sample to give the stylist a good idea of the look you're hoping to create.

Don't buy your tiara or veil until you've spoken to your hairdresser – his or her input can be invaluable.

HAIR CHECKLIST

These are some general guidelines to ensure that your hair looks fabulous on the big day!

- Book your appointment in advance. It's not uncommon for a good hairdresser to be booked up for months ahead.
- Have at least one style rehearsal a month before the wedding. This will give you time to make alternative arrangements should you be less than thrilled.
- Be honest with your stylist. You should feel comfortable expressing what you do and don't like.
- Leave plenty of time for your appointment – $2\frac{1}{2}$ hours should do it. This is not a day to rush!

- Get your hair in tip-top shape. Plan regular weekly visits to the salon for trims and conditioning treatments two months before the wedding.
- If you've given nature a little hand with the hue of your locks, colour your hair three weeks before the ceremony to prevent roots showing and to give the colour time to settle.
- Don't expect too much from your hair. If you have fine, flyaway hair, asking for voluptuous tresses is just plain unrealistic.
- Keep in mind that your style has to last the entire day.
- Don't experiment on your wedding day – it'll all end in tears.

BEAUTY COUNTDOWN

12 weeks to go	Facial, including eyebrow shape Neck and back massage Waxing Hair cut for wedding style	Deep cleansing for the skin and shaping eyebrows to complement the face. Finish with a relaxing massage to unwind. This is your chance to decide on your wedding style and start styling your hair towards it.
10 weeks to go	Manicure and pedicure	Strengthening and conditioning nails as well as moisturizing skin on hands and feet.
7 weeks to go	Facial Neck and back massage Waxing	Anti-ageing and moisturizing for the skin. Eyebrows should now be the correct shape. Have another relaxing massage!
5 weeks to go	Manicure and pedicure	Experiment with nail colours.
3 weeks to go	Hair cut and colour	Have a final trim before your big day. If you are having your hair coloured, do it now so it has time to settle down.
1 week to go	Facial Neck and back massage Waxing	You should be seeing the results of regular facials. Don't miss the massage!
2 days to go	Manicure and pedicure Trial make-up	Final shaping of nails and conditioning skin – paint toenails. Establish the make-up look that suits you.
Wedding day	Make-up Nail varnish Hair	Paint fingernails and toenails first and make sure they dry completely. Set aside plenty of time for doing your hair and make-up.

Transport & flowers

Transport

The journey to your wedding venue may be one of the most nerve-wracking and emotional of your life, and the trip to your reception may be the most wonderful, so there's every reason to do both in style and/or comfort. Push the boat out – literally, if you want to!

The style of your wedding will dictate the type of transport you choose, but keep in mind that anything fancy will come with a fancy price tag. Besides your budget, you'll need to consider practical issues carefully. Arriving by hot air balloon is not the ideal time to discover your paralyzing fear of heights.

Before deciding on your mode of transport, consider the style of your wedding, distances involved, time of journey and time of year. For example, a horse-drawn carriage is romantic, but inappropriate for a long journey in winter. One last thing: make sure that your groom doesn't make arrangements for something unusual without consulting you.

The options

Although a vintage Rolls or Daimler is the traditional and certainly the most glamorous way to arrive at your wedding, there are some weird and wonderful alternatives!

Classy motor A stretch limousine adds a dash of Hollywood glamour to the proceedings and you'll feel like a star. Alternatively, plump for a classic American car like a 1950s Cadillac in a funky colour like bubblegum pink! If the pair of you are sports car fanatics, why not hire a spectacular set of wheels and roll up in a racy Ferrari, Porsche, Aston Martin – or even matching Mini Coopers à la *Italian Job?*

Find the chariot of your dreams in your area by clicking on: *www.confetti.co.uk/ weddingplanner/p100*

My little pony (and trap) Fulfil your fantasies of the perfect fairy-tale wedding by drawing up in a horse and carriage. Intensely romantic and very picturesque, this mode of transport is perfect for a country wedding where you won't have to negotiate busy roads.

Chopper's away For an entrance worthy of a Bond girl, arrive by helicopter. This is not only a thrilling way to travel, but it can also be very practical, especially if your ceremony venue is some way from your home or the reception. But this is one to avoid if you're a nervous flyer, worried about crushing your dress or messing up your hair, or on a tight budget!

On foot If you live very close to the venue of your ceremony, why not walk there?

Drive your own If you're passionate about your own car, why not use it on the big day?

Water berth For a wedding in a riverside hotel, arrive by boat.

Marriage à la Mod If you're marrying abroad, say on a Greek island, zip into your ceremony on Vespa scooters, hired locally.

Cabbing it A white Hackney cab is an inexpensive, practical and very stylish way to be transported to your wedding.

Something on the side For a cute and quirky means of transport, try a vintage motorbike and sidecar.

TRANSPORT CHECKLIST

- Which journeys will you need transport for?
- How will the groom, best man and members of the wedding party travel to the ceremony?
- Is transport for guests required?
- Choose transport that's in keeping with the style of your wedding.
- Make sure you see the vehicle before booking or paying a deposit – photos and leaflets don't show marks, dents or a scruffy interior.
- How much does the company charge? Is there a minimum charge?
- Is a standard wedding package offered? Is there a discount when booking extra vehicles?
- Are decorations and champagne included? Can these be left out in exchange for an upgraded vehicle?
- Are the drivers/operators certified?
- What will they wear?
- What kind of licensing/insurance do they have?
- What is the contingency plan should your vehicle not be available?
- How far in advance will you have to make your booking?
- What is the company's policy on cancellation/postponement?
- How much is the deposit to secure the date and when is it due?
- When is the balance due?
- Is VAT included in the final price?
- Confirm dates, times and locations with a written contract, and reconfirm any bookings you make the week before the wedding.
- Get insurance.
- Choose a wedding car in a colour that doesn't clash with the bride's bouquet or the bridesmaids' dresses.
- Buy the ribbon for the car in advance and ask a reliable (and handy) member of the bridal party to attach it on the day. This can be fiddly to do, so practice is essential.
- Colour coordinate the car ribbon with your flowers and/or the colour theme of your wedding.
- If you're using your own car or borrowing one, have it valeted – you don't want to have to scramble over empty crisp packets or end up sitting on the dog's blanket!
- Make sure you can easily enter/exit the vehicle in your dress?
- Have a bottle of champagne chilling on ice in the back of the vehicle for a post-ceremony celebratory drink.

Wedding flowers

Deciding on the flowers for your wedding needs to be done at about the same time as you arrange your transport – well in advance and at least six months before the wedding. Choose varieties to complement the style of your day, and enlist the help of someone who knows what they're doing.

A question of money

Make sure that you allow enough money to pay for all the flowers you want. Do your research thoroughly – you'll probably be very surprised at how much flowers cost!

Normally, the groom pays for the bride's bouquet, buttonholes, corsages and the flowers for the bridesmaids, while the bride's parents pay for the ceremony and reception flowers. Remember to get a written quotation from your florist well in advance and make sure that it covers all the extras, including floral headdresses, and thank you bouquets for the mothers, if you're having them.

Flowers for the wedding party

The bride usually carries a bouquet and wears flowers in her hair or a 'crown' of flowers to hold her veil in place. Be careful when choosing flowers for buttonholes, corsages and hair. They should be wired or preserved, or they may wilt before the day is out.

The bride's flowers set the tone and scheme for the bridesmaids' bouquets, the buttonholes for the groom, best man, ushers and father of the bride, and the corsages for the couple's mothers. The tradition of a flower girl strewing petals along the aisle of the church for the bride to step on dates from the Middle Ages. Very sweet, but check first that your officiant approves!

Church flowers

The most usual positions for flower arrangements in the church are the chancel steps, the windowsills and the pew-ends. Some clergymen will allow the altar to be decorated; others are strongly opposed to the idea.

Your celebrant may suggest that the floral decorations be left to those who arrange the church flowers every week. The advantage of this is that they are more conversant with the layout of the church and where flowers show to the best advantage. However, if you're not happy with this arrangement, a little tactful negotiation will need to take place – after all, you'll be paying for the flowers and possibly the arranger, too!

Find out if another wedding service is taking place on the same day as yours. If so, it makes sense for the brides to make contact with each other and discuss the flowers they would both like to have and perhaps arrange to share the cost. You could always ask for your flowers to be given to a local hospital, old people's home or wherever you feel they will be appreciated after the ceremony (and usually after the Sunday service is over!).

Register office flowers

Many register offices change their flowers every day, since
ceremonies can take place whenever it is open. However, you
may be allowed to bring in a special arrangement, if you wish.

Reception flowers

Flower arrangements here are very much determined by the
venue and the kind of reception you are having. It's nice for guests
waiting in line to see an arrangement of flowers nearby. Other
arrangements can be placed around the hall or marquee. Smaller
displays on individual tables add an air of festivity and charm.

If a hall or rooms are being hired for the reception, flowers
are sometimes included in the reception hire package. Make sure
they will be to your liking and match your colour scheme. Again,
there might be an opportunity to share the costs with a bride
who is holding a reception in the same place the day before or
the day after yours.

Many couples prefer to use fresh flowers to adorn their
wedding cake rather than artificial ones, or plastic figures or
models such as horseshoes.

The bouquet

Wedding flowers are nothing new. Roman brides and grooms
both wore garlands of flowers to symbolize new life and fertility,
and, more recently, brides wore orange blossoms in their hair to
represent purity and fruitfulness. During Victorian times, lovers
sent each other flowers to convey different qualities and
emotions (see page 107). These associations were adopted for
brides' bouquets and some brides still use them today.

MATCHING THE SEASON

These days you can find almost any kind of flower at any time of the year, but you may prefer something to suit the season of your wedding.

- **Spring** daffodils, narcissi, bluebells, freesias, tulips, hyacinths
- **Summer** roses, hydrangeas, stephanotis, lisianthus, sunflowers, sweet peas, delphiniums, larkspur
- **Autumn** chrysanthemums, wheat, euphorbia, hypericum berries, alstromeria, gerbera
- **Winter** ivy, lilies, orchids, hippeastrum, dark red roses, dendrobium

Most brides like to include their favourite flowers in their bouquet, but the style of the wedding dress and colours she and the rest of the wedding party will be wearing are the most important aspects to be considered.

There are many different types of bridal bouquet, from a wild flower posy to a basket of flowers, a single amazing lily stem or a traditional sheaf of varied blooms. Some brides even choose a freeze-dried bouquet, which lasts forever. There are many companies who will preserve your fresh flower bouquet, too.

Whatever flowers you decide on, keep your arrangements to scale with the venue and occasion. A grand wedding requires more stylized floral arrangements, while a small reception at home could be adequately catered for with simple vase arrangements and bunches of flowers.

Finding a florist

To search for a florist in your area, click on: www.confetti.co.uk/ weddingplanner/p106

You need to decide whether to employ a professional florist or get family or a friend to do some floral DIY. Don't forget that most of the arranging will need to be done immediately before the wedding – a time when things are at their most hectic – so don't rope in a key member of the bridal party. They won't thank you for it!

If you don't already have a florist in mind, by far the best method for choosing one is by recommendation. Standards of service vary considerably. Always ask to see photos of other wedding flower arrangements that the florist has done.

The price of flowers can be alarming and much depends on seasonal availability, so to cut costs find out what's in season (see page 105) and work round it. When visiting a florist, take as much information with you as possible to help them to help you. If possible, take sketches of your dress, the attendants' clothes and samples of the fabrics. You could also cut out pictures of the kinds of bouquet you particularly like. All this will help the florist achieve the best possible result for your special day. A good florist will ask to visit the church or register office and the reception venue if you've hired them to decorate those as well.

THE LANGUAGE OF FLOWERS

Flower	Meaning
bluebell	everlasting love
carnation	fascination
chrysanthemum	truth
daffodil	regard
daisy	sharing/innocence
flowering almond	hope
forget-me-not	speaks for itself!
heather (white)	luck
heliotrope	devotion
honeysuckle	generosity
iris	flame
ivy	fidelity
japonica	loveliness
lemon blossom	fidelity in love
lilac	youthful innocence
lily	purity/majesty
lily-of-the-valley	return of happiness
mimosa	sensitivity
myrtle	love
orange blossom	purity
peach blossom	captive
rose (pale pink)	grace
rose (red)	passion
rose (white)	love and beauty
rosemary	remembrance
snowdrop	hope
stephanotis	exotic travel
sweet pea	pleasure
tulip	love
veronica	fidelity
violet	fidelity

Picture perfect

Photography

Your wedding day will never be repeated, so it's vital to have a photographer who can capture all the best moments without cutting anyone's head off or giving you 'red eye'.

Finding the right photographer

Start your search for a photographer early because good ones get booked up a long time in advance. And before you make your final choice, try to visit at least three photographers – check out their studio and staff and don't be afraid to ask questions. Ask to see full wedding album samples and make sure that the photos you're shown are the work of the person who will be taking your wedding pictures, not simply the best photos from the studio.

It's important to check credentials. Check if the photographer is a qualified member of MPA (Master Photographers Association), BIPP (British Institute of Professional Photographers) or Guild of Wedding Photographers.

Whoever you book to take your pictures will be spending a substantial amount of time with you on the best day of your lives, so you must get on with him or her and feel confident and relaxed in their presence. If you don't feel comfortable, this will be reflected in the final images.

Is the price right?

Prices range from anything upwards of £500, and wedding photography is one area where you really do get what you pay for. Most photographers have a menu of prices and will charge you a flat rate for taking shots on the day, plus an additional charge based on how many photographs you want in your album.

THE SHOOT LIST

Before the big day, discuss a rough shoot list with your photographer. The traditional choices include:

- groom and best man outside the church/civil venue
- bride's arrival at the church/civil venue
- bride and father walking down the aisle/bride entering the civil venue

- bride and groom at the altar/desk
- exchange of rings
- signing of the church register/documentation
- procession out of the church/civil venue
- group shots outside the church/civil venue
- arriving at the reception
- cutting the cake

The quality of the albums on offer (leather, plastic, velvet) can vary enormously and this will affect the cost as well. Remember that your family will be charged separately for any copies they want. Look for those nice little extras, though – some photographers will include thank you cards with a small photo enclosed as part of the deal.

Put it on paper

Once you've found the right photographer and decided on a style, get your booking in writing. Check the small print and make sure you know exactly what you're getting for your money. You could even ask the photographer to sign a contract that records your wedding date, time and place, price and any restrictions or conditions.

You will also want to ascertain when the proofs will be ready and how long you can keep them to make your selection. Find out exactly when your album will be ready, too.

Think style & colour

There are lots of ways for your photographer to record your wedding, from the traditional posed group shots to more candid reportage-style shots, such as the bride in her curlers. Most couples choose a combination of styles and film.

If you want a complete formal record of the whole wedding, it's best to go for traditional photographs. Couples seeking a more relaxed, unposed album, on the other hand, should choose reportage style. If you've spent a long time creating invitations, menus, flower arrangements and the like, you'll want a photographer who will capture these little details on film, too.

You'll need to decide whether to go for black-and-white or colour photographs. Couples who have carefully colour coordinated their day will want photos that record their creation. Black-and-white, meanwhile, creates a more timeless image. Some photographers will agree to do a combination.

Many couples place disposable cameras on the table(s) at the reception for guests to take their own pictures of the celebrations. Ask guests to leave the cameras behind at the end of the evening for you to develop the films. The photos will give you a unique insight into your day from other people's points of view!

To buy disposable cameras online, click on: *www.confetti.co.uk/ weddingplanner/p111*

Meeting up

Try to meet up at the venues for the service and the reception beforehand, so that the photographer can get a feel for the best settings to enhance the style of photographs. Remember that you need to check with your minister to make sure photography is permitted during the wedding ceremony.

A good professional photographer will use his or her creative and technical skills to get the best results as quickly, smoothly and tactfully as possible, but discuss the role you want your photographer to undertake on your wedding day. Do you want him or her to control events or blend into the background? One well-known photographer likes to shepherd guests into position with the help of a shrill whistle. It's not very subtle, but it breaks the ice and no one misses out on any of the photo calls.

Relax!

Try to relax in front of the camera. If you're not used to smiling and posing, or feel unhappy with your usual image in pictures, grab a mirror and spend a few minutes practising until you find a smile or an expression you can live with. If you look and feel comfortable, your photos are bound to work!

Remember to stand up straight with your head back, no double chins, and smile – a lot of cameras, not to mention video recorders, are going to be aimed at you and you'll want all the pictures of the day to catch you looking your best. Have a glass of champagne before you walk up the aisle – it will relax you beautifully for the camera.

Video star!

For many brides and grooms, that special day passes in a bit of a blur – a flurry of fleeting conversations, photos and having to be in all places at once. But a wedding video can provide a wonderful lasting memento of the occasion, catching all those amusing incidents you missed while you were involved with the receiving line or photographs. It provides a vivid record of all your guests, the venue, the speeches and even the ceremony itself. A copy of your wedding video also makes a great gift for friends and relatives who were unable to attend.

Using a professional

For a truly slick and infinitely watchable video, you generally need to hire a professional videomaker. However, be warned: the cost can be prohibitive.

The best way to find a videomaker is through personal recommendation. Alternatively, contact the Association of Professional Videomakers. Always ask to see samples of their work so you can check the quality and style. Ask to see a video of a whole wedding, not a tape of edited highlights from several different ones. Make sure the same person who filmed the wedding you are watching will film your wedding.

Book your videomaker well in advance – the best ones get snapped up early. Ideally, you should make your booking as soon as the date and venue have been confirmed.

Once you have found the right videomaker, determine exactly what is included in the price and whether there will be extra charges for editing, adding titles and dubbing music, and whether you can choose your own music.

Obviously, the video will include key moments like cutting the cake and the first dance, but you should also let the videomaker know if there are other special moments you want captured, such as the moment your groom first sees you in your dress. If there are certain people you want included in the video, assign a bridesmaid or usher to point them out to the videomaker.

Using an amateur

If your budget won't stretch to hiring a professional videomaker, the other option is to ask a friend or relative if they would be willing to video the big day for you. Many people own camcorders or digital video cameras, and these are also readily available for hire. Obviously, an amateur video will never be as polished or perfect as a professionally made one, but it can still capture all the joy and fun of the day, albeit in a rougher and readier fashion!

Get your appointed 'cameraman' to experiment with the camera well in advance and plan with them what is to be filmed and when. Short sharp bursts of, say, 10 to 20 seconds of filming can be the most effective, especially if you get them professionally edited to music. Remember to ask your minister or registrar for permission to film the ceremony first.

An inexperienced videomaker should not rapidly zoom in and out towards people – the effect will be blurry. It's worth getting hold of a tripod and attaching the video camera for some parts of the wedding, especially the ceremony. The footage will be steadier and more professional looking. Too much footage is better than too little – the video can always be edited down.

PHOTOGRAPHY & VIDEO CHECKLIST

- Is the photographer/videomaker available before and after the ceremony, at your home and at the reception?
- How do they charge? Flat fee? By the hour?
- What kind of packages do they offer? Can you make substitutions?
- Are prints/extra videotapes included in the price? Is the cost of an album included in the price?
- Are they willing to follow a list of requested shots?
- Will they have an assistant/assistants? Is their cost included in the price?
- What will everyone be wearing?
- Are you expected to provide food and/or transportation?
- If there is an emergency, will you be sent an alternative photographer/videomaker? If yes, can you see examples of their work?
- How soon after the wedding will the proofs/tapes be available? How long can you have the proofs before you make your selection?
- How long will the photographer keep the negatives?
- Who owns the rights to the images?
- How far in advance are bookings required?
- What is their policy on cancellation/postponement?
- How much is the deposit to secure the date?
- When is the deposit due?
- How soon after the event is the balance due?
- Is VAT included in the final price?
- Confirm dates, times and locations with a written contract.
- Get insurance.

The reception

Planning the reception

This should begin as soon as you set the wedding date – usually at least three months in advance. Popular venues (or any venue on popular dates like a bank holiday) may need to be reserved up to one year before the event, so get a provisional booking in as soon as you can.

It's important that you celebrate your marriage in a style to suit you, so don't feel forced into the conventional sit-down meal in a marquee if you'd rather eat fish and chips in your local pub.

Who does what?

The bride's family is traditionally responsible for making all the reception arrangements and absorbing the cost, which can mean paying for food, drink, a wedding cake, caterers, waiting staff, a toastmaster, flower arrangements, a band or disco, entertainers or musicians and any security arrangements. Sometimes couples cover the cost of the wedding reception themselves or share it between the families. Whoever's footing the bill, it's the reception that is likely to be the single biggest expense of the wedding, so plan it carefully.

When to have your reception

The timing of your reception is really up to you. You can have a wedding breakfast, which is the traditional name for what is actually a sit-down lunch following a morning wedding ceremony. Or you can have an afternoon reception, held after a 2.30 or 3pm service. This is usually followed by an evening party/disco held some hours later, which gives everybody time to change into less formal clothes, if they wish. However, make sure that your guests, particularly those from out of town, are not left stranded with nothing to do between the end of the lunch and the beginning of the evening celebrations.

Sometimes the 'evening do' is hosted by the couple themselves and invitations are issued in their names. This is also a chance to invite people you couldn't afford to feed! The more continental late-afternoon service, followed by an evening reception with dinner and dancing, has recently become quite fashionable. Guests are invited to wear evening dress to the ceremony. If you're getting married abroad in a hot climate, a late afternoon or early morning ceremony is best, unless you want to fry!

You might find your reception timetable is partly dictated by licensing laws. You need to check how late a venue's licence extends before you make a firm booking. Even if your reception is in a hotel, where overnight guests can continue to purchase drinks legally, there may be a limit on how long the music is allowed to go on.

Choosing the venue

When women used to live at home until they were married, wedding receptions were traditionally held at the bride's family home. Today, receptions can take place almost anywhere – hotels, banqueting halls, clubs, marquees, a village hall or stately home.

The number of people you want at your reception may well dictate your choice of venue – or vice versa! It is usual for everyone who has been invited to the wedding ceremony to be asked to the reception. If only a small number of guests can attend the ceremony due to lack of space, or you want a very private ceremony, then additional guests can be invited to the reception afterwards. For 100 guests or more, consider rooms designed specifically for holding receptions, as they will have all the facilities you need.

Most reception venues will quote you a cost per head for food and drink, a hire charge for the venue (or marquee) plus the cost of any entertainment, a toastmaster, cake stand, and so on. In your initial consultation with a venue, get a full list of all the possible costs and charges. Decide roughly what your budget is and your ideal head count and then the venue price range will become clear. A venue will be able to offer you a number of services, which may include a registrar, food, drink and music as well as accommodation. Many will take a lot of the organization out of your hands and will employ a wedding coordinator or events manager.

Your venue is the place where you are going to entertain all of your friends and relations – so take your time to get it right. Start your search a long time

For some of the most beautiful reception venues, take a look at: *www.confetti.co.uk/ weddingplanner/p119*

– ideally a year – before your party as this gives you the time to make the right decision without rushing into anything.

If you're searching for something unique, you need to think laterally. You may have seen a building or even a private house that you feel would be perfect. Although some places look like they may seem unavailable, don't believe it until you have asked. Have the courage to approach a venue that looks exciting – because if you want to do something different, your venue needs to be dramatic.

Maybe a marquee?

A marquee is a good option for large gatherings, and you may like to set one up in your own garden or that of willing parents or a friend. Marquees come in a huge array of shapes, sizes, prices and specifications. Do shop around and find out what is available for the date you have chosen. Remember that your marquee will need flooring and a lining as well, which will have to be priced. You'll need to show the hire company the site to ensure that it's suitable for your requirements.

MARQUEE CHECKLIST

- Is the location close enough to the place of worship or register office?
- Will holding the reception at home increase the stress factor dramatically?
- Are lavatory and cloakroom facilities sufficient?
- Can the hire company arrange for portable toilets, if necessary?
- Will the caterers be able to function effectively in the kitchen of the home or will you need to hire a portable kitchen?
- Is there space for a bar?
- Is there sufficient parking space?
- Will the company do an on-site estimate?
- Will a marquee accommodate all your guests? Is there room to mingle? Is there room for a dance floor?
- What colour is the marquee? What types of lining are available?
- Is proper flooring available? What about staging for the speeches and entertainment?
- Is the hire of tables and chairs included in the price?
- Is there a sufficient power supply for any entertainment/sound systems you may require?
- Can the hire company provide a generator if additional electricity is needed?
- Can they provide interior lighting? Exterior lighting? Heating? A public address system for speeches/ entertainment?
- Can your theme and decorations be incorporated into the structure easily?
- Is access to permanent shelter/house available?
- Can walkways be covered?
- When will the marquee need to be set up and dismantled?
- Will someone be available on-call during the event if there are any emergencies?
- How far in advance are bookings required?
- What is the policy on cancellation/ postponement?
- How much is the deposit to secure the date? When is it due?
- How soon after the event is the balance due?
- Is VAT included in the final price?
- Confirm dates, times and details with a written contract.
- Get insurance.

Size matters!

Once you know roughly how many guests you will be inviting, you'll have a good idea of the amount of space that you will need in order to set up chairs, tables and a dance floor area. Be careful – a venue that is too spacious loses its intimacy and a venue that is too small will be cramped.

Meet the caretaker

This sounds like an off beat tip... but it's probably the most significant of all. You need to establish early on whether or not the management of your venue is on your side or not. Most are friendly and flexible, but there are certain museums and historic buildings run by caretakers/managers who are, deep down, 'anti-party' people – they would prefer to see their venues full of art or exhibits instead of wine and music.

Questions to ask

There are a number of questions to ask when you're visiting potential venues (see pages 124–5), and the answers you're given will give you a guide as to whether you will be dealing with an organization that is either efficient and flexible or inexperienced. If you like what you hear, then pay a deposit and sign a binding contract. It's also important for you to know whether you are going to be able to decorate the venue in plenty of time if you are doing it yourself, and that whoever is deputized to remove gifts, lost property, and so on, afterwards doesn't have to do it at two in the morning, but can come in the next day.

Layout

Once you have decided on your venue, you need to look ahead to the actual event. The layout of the reception area – as well as the dining/dancing area – need to be established. Drawing a plan is a good idea. Sketch in the tables, dance floor, bar and the serveries, and leave room for the stage and music equipment. When these items are in place, sketch in the decorations and play around with the plan. Remember that all of the guests are equally important, so the positioning of the tables is everything (see page 128). Everyone, wherever they are sitting, needs to feel special.

Transport & car parking

Remember to check out the parking facilities, and get the details of reliable local taxi companies, which your guests might find very useful at the end of the evening.

VENUE CHECKLIST

- Is the venue big enough to accommodate all your guests?
- Is the reception venue within a reasonable distance of the ceremony venue? How easy is it to find? Is it well sign-posted?
- Are there adequate parking facilities?
- Is there accommodation at the venue? Is there a discount for guests?
- What types of wedding package are available?
- Does the venue have an in-house wedding coordinator? How far in advance can you meet up to go over details?
- Are there any special conditions imposed by the venue?
- Are there adequate cloakroom and lavatory facilities?

- Are there facilities and special seating for less mobile guests or anyone with a disability, particularly if a sit-down meal is not included in the celebrations?
- If children are to be invited, are there any special facilities for them?
- Does the venue have equipment you can use?
- Will you have to hire tables, chairs, linen, crockery, cutlery, glassware and vases?
- Are the tables, chairs, linen and overall ambience appropriate for your style of wedding?
- Are decorations, such as flowers, included or will you have to provide your own? Discuss where you would like them.

- Can you bring in your own choice of caterer, florist, decorator and other services?
- If you are bringing in a caterer, will they have access to a kitchen, power supply and running water?
- Can the venue supply the cake stand and knife?
- Does the venue have a licence to consume alcohol? Is there a late-night curfew?
- Can you supply your own alcohol? Is there a corkage fee?
- Until what time will the bar be open?
- How will the staff be dressed? How many will be required?
- Is a toastmaster included in the staffing costs?
- Is entertainment permitted?
- Is smoking permitted?
- Is there a sufficient power supply for any entertainment/sound systems you may require?
- Is there a public address system for speeches?
- Are there noise level restrictions?
- Is the lighting suitable? Visit your venue at the time of day your reception will take place.
- Where can guests store coats and personal belongings?
- Is there a safe place for storing gifts?
- Are there other weddings booked for the same day?
- If you are having outside staff or decorators in or decorating the venue yourself, what is the earliest time you will be allowed access to the venue?
- Is there a private room in which you can change into going-away outfits?
- Can you see the room while it's being used for another wedding reception?
- Does the venue have public liability insurance?
- How far in advance are bookings required?
- What is the policy on cancellation/postponement?
- How much is the deposit to secure the date and when is it due?
- How soon after the event is the balance due?
- Is VAT included in the final price?
- Confirm dates, times and details with a written contract.
- Get insurance.

At the reception

If you've opted for a formal wedding and reception, you will obviously have a great deal of planning to do, but even the most informal receptions tend to follow a certain pattern.

The receiving line

A formal receiving line is where the bride and groom line up with both sets of parents and greet each guest as they enter the room. However, it can be just the couple that receive their guests. If both sets of parents are in the line, it is advisable to go through the guest list together before the day, so that everyone is acquainted with the guests' names.

The receiving line can be organized as the guests leave the wedding ceremony or as they arrive at the reception, which is the most popular choice. It is becoming increasingly popular for a master of ceremonies to announce each guest as they enter the room, so that everyone in the receiving line knows who they are about to speak to. The conventional way of arranging the line, based on the notion that the bride's parents are paying for the entire wedding, is to have the bride's mother and father first, then the groom's parents and then the bride and groom. You may like to add the best man and chief bridesmaid to the end of the line.

Since it's no longer the norm for the bride's parents to pay for the entire wedding, there's no reason why you have to stick to the traditional order or even have a receiving line at all. However, it does give you the chance to talk to every guest individually at least once on the day and thank them for coming.

The top table

The traditional top table for the wedding party has everyone seated down one side of a rectangular table, facing the rest of the room. The usual arrangement is, from the left: chief bridesmaid, groom's father, bride's mother, groom, bride, bride's father, groom's mother, best man (see above).

An alternative to this is to swap the fathers so that the bride's parents sit together and the groom's parents sit together. Whether you split the parents and put them with each other's partner or not is up to you. It's less and less common to have a formal seating arrangement on the top table, so go with what will make everyone happiest. Remember that the top table is always the focus of attention, and any resentment or bitterness lurking between people, for example current partners and exes, is going to be very obvious.

If you have large numbers of extended family, you might need to be a little more creative with your 'top table' arrangement. A round (non-hierarchical) table is always a good way to solve this problem. But who says all the leading players in your wedding have to sit together anyway? You could set up several tables, rather than just the one top table.

While it's best to avoid seating sworn enemies next to each other, sometimes it's unavoidable. If this happens, warn each person in advance and trust that their love for you will take precedence over their mutual animosity. It's important to remember that the onus is on others to cooperate and be at least civil to one another. It's not for you to come up with the seating plan from heaven that will magically wipe out all tension. Of course you want people to get on and be happy on your special day, but don't let their issues become yours.

Where do the guests sit?

The seating plan for the meal is based on the idea of intermingling the two families, but many people organize their seating plans so that guests have familiar faces around them.

Keep track of who's sitting where with an interactive personalized table planner at: www.confetti.co.uk/weddingplanner/p128

Sorting out the seating plan is not an easy task. Tact and a good knowledge of the guests are vital. It is also worth remembering that weddings can be a reunion for friends and relatives who normally do not have an opportunity to meet. It's also where old enemies may come face to face again!

The layout of your tables is a personal choice. Some like the idea of an elongated top table, where extensions are added at right angles to both ends of the top table. Guests can be seated on both sides of these side tables. Alternatively, individual round tables can be arranged for the guests.

No matter how hard you try, you might end up with a seating plan with tables of people who've never met before. If you're worried that your tables are too 'mixed' and you need an icebreaker, why not place quizzes about the bride and groom on all the tables?

For specially packaged wedding and romance trivia quizzes, click on: *www.confetti.co.uk/ weddingplanner/p129*

You should discuss the layout of the tables with the hotel staff or catering firm and agree the seating plan well in advance. On the day, the seating plan can be placed on an easel for the guests to see as they come in for the meal, and there should be corresponding place cards on the tables. If you have a lot of guests, set up several easels so that everyone can check their seat number easily without causing a crowd to build up.

Speeches & toasts

Most receptions include speeches and toasts. These should always be properly planned, rehearsed and timed. Usually they come at the end of the meal, although there is an increasing trend to have them before the meal begins. Usually, the father of the bride speaks and then toasts the bride and groom. Next comes the groom – and perhaps the bride. They thank their guests for coming and, traditionally, the groom proposes a toast to the bridesmaids. Then, finally, comes the best man, who officially 'replies' on behalf of the bridesmaids.

For inspirational favours available online, visit: *www.confetti.co.uk/ weddingplanner/p130*

Do them a favour

It's usual nowadays to give each guest a tiny gift, or favour, to remind them of the wedding day. These range from traditional Italian sugared almonds, more modern confectionery options, such as chocolates or jelly beans, to perfumed candles, even extravagant silver trinkets.

Cutting the cake

The bride and groom cut the cake together as a symbol of their shared future. After the cake cutting ceremony (usually at the very end of the meal and after the speeches), the caterers remove the cake, which is sliced up and handed round to guests.

First dance

The evening is the time for everyone to relax and enjoy themselves and, maybe, go wild on the dance floor! Traditionally, the bride and groom have the 'first dance' together. This would have been a waltz in the past, but nowadays it's whatever you choose. If you don't relish the idea of dancing in public, open the dance floor to everyone as soon as the music starts.

It is also traditional for the groom to dance with his new mother-in law and then with his mother, while the bride dances with her new father-in law and then her father. The best man joins in by dancing with the chief bridesmaid, while the ushers dance with the other bridesmaids.

Time to go home?

Guests are supposed to remain at the reception until the couple leave, so if there is to be no formal 'going away', let your guests know (especially the older ones) that you intend to dance the night away!

Throwing it all away

After the reception, the bride throws her bouquet over her shoulder towards a group of her unmarried girlfriends and female relatives. Traditionally, the one who catches the flowers (and survives the scrum!) will be the next to marry.

Lights, music, action!

The entertainment you have at your wedding offers an unrivalled opportunity for flights of fancy and extravagance. On the other hand, you can keep it simple and affordable. At your daytime reception, you could hire, say, a harpist and flute duo, a string quartet or a small jazz band to make some pretty background noise. Their repertoire should be light enough to appeal to a varied age group and never so loud that it overwhelms the conversation.

The evening entertainment is a matter of personal choice. Anything goes, from karaoke to a live orchestra, from a jazz band to a raging disco. Just bear in mind the age range of your guests and the layout of the venue.

From ceilidhs to discos, the entertainment is a vital part of the celebrations and often takes up a big part of the evening. Ensure that you have heard or seen any entertainers. Bands might send tapes or invitations to hear them play, and DJs should allow you to choose many or all of the songs played. Alternatively, entertainment agents can arrange everything for you. Reputable agents should be registered with either The Entertainment Agents Association of Great Britain or The National Entertainment Agents Council. You might want to consider alternative entertainment, such as magicians, casino games and fireworks.

ENTERTAINMENT CHECKLIST

- What type of entertainment would you like? DJ? Dance band? Cover band?
- How do they charge? Do they offer any special packages or discounts? Is there a minimum time requirement? Will they play overtime and at what cost? Are travel costs included?
- Will you be responsible for feeding the entertainers?
- Do they have a demo tape you can listen to?
- Where can you hear them perform live?
- In the case of a band, how long have these particular musicians been playing together and performing at weddings?
- What time will they arrive? How long will it take to set up?
- How often do they take breaks and how long are they?
- Can arrangements be made for taped music to be played during breaks?
- What will they be wearing?
- Does the venue have an entertainment licence?
- Can the volume be easily controlled?

- Does the DJ work from a predetermined playlist?
- Are you able to pass on a list of songs you do or don't want?
- Are they able to accommodate requests?
- Is there any equipment you will need to supply?
- How far in advance are bookings required?
- What is the policy on cancellation/postponement?
- How much is the deposit to secure the date and when is it due?
- How soon after the event is the balance due?
- Is VAT included in the final price?
- Confirm dates, times and details with a written contract.
- Get insurance.

Food & drink

Once you've found your ideal venue, you and your fiancé and/or your parents should make an appointment with the person in charge to discuss dates, times, numbers of guests, the catering and the exact price of everything.

The catering and refreshments will very much depend on the venue and type of reception you have decided to organize. Some venues may have resident caterers, others may be able to recommend caterers or may even insist that you use a particular one. However, for a low-key affair, local restaurants, bakers, off-licences and even supermarkets will be more than willing to give you an estimate. Seriously consider a professional caterer if your guest list exceeds 20, then you won't have to worry about dirty dishes and whether or not everyone has had enough to eat. Hire staff to serve and clear up – it's money well spent. It's probably best not to accept offers of help from invited guests – after all, they are meant to be celebrating with you!

If you need help finding a caterer for your wedding, click on: www.confetti.co.uk/weddingplanner/p134

Choosing a caterer

It is important to allow yourself sufficient time to get various estimates and to compare catering services, facilities and costs, if necessary. Remember that good caterers tend to get booked up months in advance.

A personal recommendation or your own experience of a caterer's work is always the best guide. If the caterer runs a restaurant or hotel, try to sample a meal on the premises before making your decision. Many hotels will let you sample their suggested wedding menus, either for free or at a reduced price, once you have made your booking with them.

Your caterer will need to know the date, time of reception, number of guests, level of hospitality you wish to provide and your limit on charges per head in order to supply you with ideas and quotations. Always ask for quotations and confirmation of everything in writing – and file your copies carefully!

And don't forget to finalize numbers with the caterers just before the wedding, especially if there are late cancellations, otherwise you'll have to pay for wasted meals.

Think about the style of reception you are having. A banquet caterer may not be appropriate for an intimate cocktail reception for 40 guests.

What to drink and when

The quantity and type of drinks provided will be determined both by the style of your meal and the number of guests. As well as alcoholic drinks, make sure there are plenty of non-alcoholic drinks, too, for children, drivers, older guests, those suffering from the heat and those suffering from too much champagne!

Drinks on arrival at the reception It is normal to provide a drink for guests as they arrive at the reception. It may be an aperitif, like a medium or dry sherry, a glass of champagne or sparkling wine, or maybe Bucks Fizz or Pimms. There should also be a soft drink on offer, such as orange juice, especially if there are children at your wedding. For a winter wedding, mulled wine is a welcome option.

HOW MUCH WINE WILL I NEED?

Use this wine calculator to help you work out how much you'll
need to buy. First, remember the following:

• You get six standard (125ml) glasses out of a standard
  (750ml or 75cl) bottle.
• Always slightly over order, allow an extra 5–10%, to cover
  any unforeseen circumstances.
• People will drink more in hot weather, but on average your
  guests should require their glasses re-filling once every
  25–30 minutes, so allow two glasses per hour, per person.

$$\frac{\text{people drinking}}{\text{glasses per bottle}} \times \begin{array}{c} \text{glasses per person} \\ \text{(@ 1 glass per person} \\ \text{each 30 minutes)} \end{array} + 10\% = \begin{array}{c} \text{total no.} \\ \text{of bottles} \\ \text{required} \end{array}$$

Example: How many bottles of champagne should you order to
keep 120 guests happy for two hours at a formal wedding in high
summer?

Answer:

$$\frac{120}{6} \times 4 + 10\% = 88$$

In view of the fact that it could well be a warm day and people
will be wearing smart outfits, which may consist of several layers
of clothing, they're likely to drink more. You should err on the side
of caution and order another 10%. This means you'll be buying
8 cases of 12 bottles, which adds up to 96 bottles.

Drinks with the meal At the meal itself, either champagne or sparkling wine can be served, but it is quite normal to have white or red wine, and often a bottle of each is placed on every table. Soft drinks should also be provided, such as orange juice or a more exotic non-alcoholic cocktail. It is also usual for bottles of water to be provided, possibly still and sparkling. If you're having an afternoon reception, you might also want to serve tea or coffee at some point.

Drinks for the toasts It is traditional for a glass of champagne to be served to each guest prior to the speeches, so that they can toast the bride and groom. Alternatively, you could serve sparkling wine.

Drinks in the evening If the celebrations go on into the evening, the hosts can arrange for drinks to be provided at their expense. It's quite acceptable to have a paying bar and for the bridal party to put some money behind it. Once that's been spent, guests pay for their own drinks.

Corkage

Your caterer or venue may provide the drinks, service and the necessary equipment, but do watch the price. Some venues allow the wedding organizer to provide the drink, but they tend to charge corkage, so you may not save much.

If you do arrange to buy drink from a supplier, such as an off-licence, make sure you get it on a sale or return basis. Usually suppliers can advise on the best choice of wines and provide glasses, ice buckets and ice.

The menu

There is no 'right' menu for a wedding meal. You can have anything you like, from a light lunch to an elaborate dinner. After initial discussions and a briefing from you, a good caterer will suggest sample menus and help you with your decision.

You could go for a finger buffet, which means that the guests do not require cutlery and are free to mingle and eat at the same time. The buffet could include canapés, small sandwiches, individual pastries and dips.

A fork buffet can be a wide choice of food with a variety of salads and/or hot dishes. The guests serve themselves and then sit at specific places laid out for them on a seating plan.

A sit-down meal is the traditional reception fare, but it is also the most expensive option. Usually there will be a minimum of three courses – starter, main course and dessert – plus coffee and wedding cake.

Let them eat (wedding) cake

You don't have to have a wedding cake at all, but it is traditional for the couple to formally 'cut' it while everyone looks on and cheers. In fact, it is an age-old symbol of fertility!

The traditional wedding cake is a rich fruit cake with thick icing. It's usually square or round and comes in two or three tiers. But there's nothing stopping you from choosing a rich chocolate or gooey lemon cake, a tower of profiteroles, even trifle!

Ordering your cake

Make sure that you order your wedding cake in good time – a multi-tiered cake can take months to create and it will need to be made and iced in different stages. Flowers generally form the main cake decorations (whether real, fabric or piped in icing), although some couples like to include balloons, ribbons or horseshoes and figurines.

When ordering your cake, your options are:
- Buy a standard cake (and have it specially decorated).
- Have it made by a specialist.
- Have it made by a relative or friend and then iced professionally.
- Have it made and iced by a relative or friend.
- Order it from the local bakery.

Get me to the cake on time

It is best for the cake to be delivered to the reception venue unassembled and then the tiers put together in situ. Make sure your venue has somewhere safe to store the cake and that they can assemble it for you.

FOOD & DRINK CHECKLIST

- Will you be having finger food, a buffet or a sit-down meal?
- Does the caterer offer any special packages? What is included?
- Is the caterer flexible with menu choices? Can you make suggestions? Will they cater for people with special dietary needs, providing vegetarian, vegan or kosher alternatives? Will they be able to cater for children?
- How soon can you have a menu tasting?
- What kind of kitchen facilities will be required?
- Are they able to work creatively within your budget?
- Is the serving staff included in the price? What is the ratio of staff to guests? What will the staff wear?
- Have they catered a wedding at your venue before?
- If catering at the bride's home, what kitchen facilities are required and will they take care of all the clearing up?
- How many other bookings do they have for the same day?
- Do they provide all necessary china, glassware and utensils?
- If rental equipment is necessary, who is responsible for its delivery, cleaning and return?
- Will your contact be at the reception to oversee the event?
- When is the final guest count due? Can they accommodate unexpected guests? What is the additional charge?
- What brands of beverages will be served?
- Can you supply your own alcohol? Is there a corkage fee?
- Will you have a free bar or will guests pay for their own beverages?
- Determine which drinks you would like served when (for example, kir royales on arrival, wine with dinner, champagne for speeches, etc).
- Will the caterer supply extra bar stock like ice, fresh lemons/limes, etc.?
- Do they have the correct glassware for the beverages you will be serving?
- Discuss table layout, seating arrangements and the position of the cake table.
- Can they provide staff to look after the cloakroom, place name cards for seating arrangements and distribute party favours?

- Is a service charge included or are gratuities optional? Is there a charge for any breakages?
- How far in advance are bookings required?
- How much is the deposit to secure the date and when is it due?
- How soon after the event is the balance due?
- Is VAT included in the final price?
- What is the policy on cancellation/postponement?
- Confirm dates, times and details with a written contract. Include a breakdown of charges for food, drinks, corkage, staff, delivery, travel expenses, equipment hire and service charges.
- Get insurance.

For the wedding cake
- What type of cake would you like: traditional fruitcake, sponge cake, etc?
- How would you like your cake presented? Flat or tiered? Round or square? Individual cakes?
- How will it be eaten? With fingers or forks? Served or taken home?
- Consider the decorations. Will you need fresh flowers or sugar paste? A cake topper? Ribbon?
- How and when will the cake be delivered? Is there a delivery charge?
- Are there appropriate refrigeration facilities on site?
- Are the decorations edible? Are any of your guests allergic to nuts?
- How far in advance should you order the cake?
- How much is the deposit to secure the date and when is it due?
- How soon after the event is the balance due?
- Is VAT included in the final price?
- What is the policy on cancellation/postponement?
- Confirm dates, times and details with a written contract.
- Get insurance.

The honeymoon

The organization

With all the wedding preparations in full swing, chances are the last thing you want to take on is more planning and organization. But for a honeymoon to remember – for the best reasons – it's worth taking a little time to get it right.

Who does what?

Many brides get their husbands to plan and book the honeymoon, for the simple reason that they are usually doing everything else! Traditionally, the groom should foot the bill as well – although most couples now simply share costs. If the groom plans a surprise trip, make sure he gives you an idea of what to expect so that you'll know what to pack and can plan to have all the necessary documentation and vaccinations.

However, for many couples, planning the trip of a lifetime is one of the most exciting parts of the pre-wedding experience and something they can do without family interference. So even if the groom takes on the research, make it a joint venture and enjoy it.

It takes two

What do you *both* want to do? Make sure that neither of you is simply agreeing to two weeks on a beach to keep the other happy. Remember, too, that you don't have to follow other people's preconceptions about honeymoons. 'Whatever makes you happy' is truly the key.

Think about money. In many ways, it's far better to choose a honeymoon that you can easily afford and have enough spending money once you're actually there rather than having to count your pennies all the time.

The options available
A quiet, relaxing time together – anywhere would do If all you're really after is time together and the stress of long-haul flights isn't your scene, then a remote cottage in Britain may serve you far better than an expensive, all-inclusive, Far Eastern beach holiday.

A little bit of luxury and privacy If you want something glamorous and gorgeous, then saving on travel in favour of a top-class location may be the best bet. For example, take the train to France and stay in a succession of luxurious châteaux and hotels.

A taste of adventure Whether you choose an African safari, white-water rafting, diving or trekking, make sure you book through a reputable company and that any dangerous activities are properly supervised.

To see the sights Perhaps you can think of nothing more romantic than being in St Mark's Square, Venice, or seeing the pyramids. Make sure you do your research and that you know what you can visit and when.

Sun, sea and sand Walking hand-in-hand through the surf on a white sandy beach is surely the definitive honeymoon scene. Just be sure – especially if you are active types – that you really do both want to be lazing around for the duration of your stay. However, it's possible for many beach holidays to build in some separate activities, and there's no reason why one of you can't scuba dive while the other sunbathes.

Action! An activity element – perhaps walking, skiing or cycling – can be perfect if you both love the activity involved. After all the stress of the wedding – and all that food and drink! – some decent exercise can be invigorating and restorative.

Best of both worlds Honeymoons are supposed to be romantic – but even the most intense lovebirds need some variety! The most popular honeymoon choice nowadays is a 'dual centre' break, combining a week of beach-based relaxation with a more active or city-based week.

Two's company... Think carefully before inviting family and friends along on your honeymoon – this is a very special time in your married life and you won't get it again.

Perfect timing

As soon as you have set your wedding date, turn your attention to the honeymoon. You should aim to book it as soon as possible, especially if you're getting married during a peak holiday season, such as July/August or Christmas/New Year.

If you're about to splash out on a 'once in a lifetime' trip, you might even want to set the honeymoon date first. But bear in mind that, although the majority of British weddings take place in June, July and August, this may not be the best time to travel to your chosen destination.

Traditionally, the blushing bride and groom take leave of their guests in the early evening and head off on honeymoon immediately, but most modern couples like to enjoy the whole reception and spend their first night together in a nearby hotel.

Budget or bust

Don't underestimate how exhausted you'll be once the wedding is over. You'll need a good break and it's worth paying a little more to stay somewhere decent. For this reason, last-minute bargain breaks are not really a good idea, unless you really don't mind when and where the honeymoon takes place! Planning well in advance may cost a bit more, but it means you'll get what you really want, when you want it.

Don't add extra stress to the trip by leaving too many elements to chance. Delays are more likely on chartered flights, so you're better off spending your money on scheduled flights instead. You don't want to spend your first night as husband and wife in a departure lounge! Book at least the first week's accommodation up front, plan the itinerary and book your car hire or internal flights. You can even plan and book activities, such as city tours or scuba diving, in advance. Search online for the local tourist board and get some ideas of what you can do while you're away.

You can book the perfect honeymoon abroad at: www.confetti.co.uk/weddingplanner/p146

Travel insurance is important for peace of mind. Should one of you fall ill, or a theft occur, you'll be covered. Make sure your policy covers the value of wedding and engagement rings. If you're marrying abroad as well, take out a special wedding policy, which will cover your wedding outfits and gifts.

Build lots of spending money into your budget, so you can indulge in a little luxury. There's not much difference between a four- and five-star hotel – spend the money you save on having fun.

HONEYMOON CHECKLIST

Three months before the wedding

- By this time you should have booked any flights/package holidays and arranged travel insurance.
- Draw up a basic itinerary and book at least the first few days' accommodation.
- Make sure your passports are valid. If you are changing your name and want to travel in your married name, contact the passport office for the necessary forms to complete.
- Obtain visas, if required.
- Have all the necessary vaccinations and check whether you need to take malaria tablets.

One month before the wedding

- Finalize your itinerary, pre-book activities, if desired, and confirm hotels in writing.
- Arrange transport from your first-night hotel to the airport and from the airport to home on your return, if applicable.
- Order your foreign currency and travellers' cheques.

- Collect all the necessary paperwork (tickets, passports, addresses and phone numbers of hotels, driver's licence, insurance details) and file it together in a safe place.
- Plan your packing.
- Arrange for someone to collect your wedding clothes from the first-night hotel and store them, or return them to the hire shops.
- Make arrangements for someone to look after your wedding presents – honeymooning newlyweds are often prime targets for break-ins.

One week before the wedding

- Collect your currency and travellers' cheques.

One day before the wedding

- Pack and have your luggage taken to the first-night hotel or other convenient point for collection.

After the wedding

Thank you letters

Letters of thanks should be prompt, personal and thoughtful.
They may be written by either the bride or groom, or both,
usually whoever is closer to the person giving the present. If you
have been given cash gifts, it's polite to indicate to the giver how
you plan to use the money, or, if you have vouchers, what you
have bought or intend to buy with them.

Exchanging gifts

If you change your mind about any items you have been given,
many gift list companies will let you exchange what you chose
previously for other items of equal value.

Give that back!

If you call off your wedding, all the presents that you have already
received should be offered back to the giver with thanks. No
detailed explanations are necessary.

Changing your name

When a woman marries, she is faced with having to make a
decision about her name. That is, should she change her maiden
name (her surname before marriage) and, if so, to what?

There is no legal requirement for a woman to change her
surname when she gets married. Upon marriage, there are two
automatic legal options available to the woman: she can either
continue to use her maiden name or she can change her maiden
name to her husband's surname. If a woman decides to take her
husband's surname, the marriage certificate provides the
necessary documentary evidence that she has changed her name.

You can change your name by deed poll at: *www.confetti.co.uk/ weddingplanner/p150*

It is also becoming increasingly popular for couples to take each other's surname after marriage. For example, if Michael Smith marries Susan Brown, they may wish to be known as Michael and Susan Smith-Brown (or Brown-Smith). Formally, the couple will be addressed as Mr and Mrs Michael Smith-Brown (the use of a hyphen between the combined surnames is optional).

If you decide upon this option and you both wish to have all your records and documents changed, you should both arrange to have your names changed by deed poll after your marriage. This will ensure that there are no delays or problems in getting all of your documents and records changed in the future.

If you choose to use a different name after your marriage, you must advise your bank, employer and other official bodies, such as the Passport Office. It is possible, though, to change the name in your passport before your wedding. This is to allow you to travel on your overseas honeymoon using your married name. To do this, you need to contact the Passport Office for the relevant forms. However, your new passport will not be valid until after you are married.

Making a will

Considering making a will at a time of joy and happiness may seem to many to be somewhat morbid and probably the furthest thing from your mind. However, the making of a will is, in fact, an act of love and consideration. It is also a responsibility undertaken by those who wish to spare their next of kin further pain of worry and even hardship when they die, especially if their death is untimely and sudden.

There are two essential prerequisites for a person to make a will: you must be at least 18 years old and be of 'sound mind'.

Any existing will is automatically revoked upon marriage, a point that has particular relevance and importance to those marrying for the second or subsequent time. The law automatically presumes that your wishes will change once you have a new spouse to consider. Therefore, any existing obligations made before the marriage will need to be readdressed to ensure that the beneficiaries are protected and that your wishes are carried out without delay and misunderstanding.

Making a will is, for most people, a simple process done through a solicitor or professional will writer. Costs are usually quite reasonable and you can expect your will to be ready within a few days. Once it is completed you can either lodge it with your solicitor or keep it in a safe place at home or even at your bank. You will need to refer to your will subsequently only if your circumstances change, such as on the birth of a child or the receipt of a large windfall.

You can even purchase do-it-yourself wills from larger stationers. These are legally binding, although they are probably only suited to those whose estate is very straightforward.

WEDDING CALENDAR

At least six months before the wedding

- Decide whether you want a religious or civil ceremony.
- Choose your church or civil venue.
- Decide on an ideal wedding date and time.
- Book service with vicar/priest/ Registrar. Check fees.
- Arrange special licence, if necessary.
- Choose reception venue.
- Buy engagement ring – if you haven't done so already!
- Agree budget with father of the bride and decide who is going to pay for what.
- Agree approximate number of guests for ceremony.
- Agree approximate number of guests for reception.
- Agree style and theme of ceremony.
- Agree style and theme of reception.
- Choose your chief bridesmaid, bridesmaids, flower girl and pageboy.
- Groom to choose his best man and ushers.
- Choose witnesses.
- Book reception venue.
- Arrange marquee, if required.
- Make catering arrangements for reception and decide on a menu.

- Book reception entertainment.
- Plan wedding outfits for the bride, bridesmaids, flower girl and pageboy.
- Book dressmaker and shoemaker.
- Order flowers, bouquets, corsages and buttonholes.
- Book photographer and videomaker.
- Draft guest list for ceremony, reception and evening celebrations.
- Book transport for wedding day and going away.
- Insure against disasters, including theft of wedding gifts.
- Book honeymoon and arrange travel insurance.
- Consider a pre-nuptial agreement.

Three months before

- Discuss church/civil ceremony and order of service with the vicar/ priest/Registrar.
- Discuss music options with the officiant and organist, if applicable.
- Book musicians and singers for ceremony.
- Select items and retailer(s) for gift list.
- Finalize gift list.
- Finalize guest list.
- Prepare map/accommodation details to send out with invitations.

- Order wedding stationery (invitations, order of service sheets, response cards, menus, napkins and place cards).
- Send out invitations with relevant enclosures.
- Create your wedding web pages, including details of the ceremony, reception, guest list, travel and accommodation.
- Buy dresses and outfits, if they're not being made.
- Bride's father and groom to decide on clothes for the men in the wedding party.
- Male members of wedding party to attend clothes fitting.
- Establish dates for publishing banns in both bride's and groom's parish, or notify appropriate register office of intended marriage.
- Buy wedding rings and arrange insurance cover.
- Book reception staff such as toastmaster, if required.
- Order/make wedding cake.
- Plan health and beauty regime, and book appointments.
- Confirm passports are up to date.
- Obtain visas, if required.

- Organize inoculations if marrying or honeymooning abroad. Check if you need to take malaria tablets
- Arrange to have your passport changed to your married name, if desired.
- Book accommodation for wedding night.

One month before
- Send out details of gift list on request.
- Send thank you letters for gifts as they arrive.
- Buy shoes, lingerie and accessories.
- Groom, father of the bride and best man to start preparing their speeches.
- If self-catering, make detailed shopping, cooking and freezing plans.
- Order reception decorations, such as balloons, and disposable cameras.
- Collect banns certificate, if marrying in local parish church.
- Check bookings: church/civil venue, florist, photographer, videomaker, transport, hotel, entertainment, cake.
- Arrange a time for wedding rehearsal.
- Buy gifts for the wedding party.

- Arrange for an announcement of your wedding to appear in the local/national press.
- Chase outstanding invitation replies for final numbers.
- Chief bridesmaid to arrange final fitting of bridesmaids' and flower girl's dresses and pageboy's outfits.
- Agree with attendants where they will dress on your wedding day.
- Have practice session with your hairdresser and make appointment for the wedding morning.
- Practise wedding day make-up.
- Chief bridesmaid to arrange hen party.
- Best man to organize stag party, with the help of the ushers, if necessary.
- Arrange safe storage for gifts brought to the reception and for someone to look after them while you're away on honeymoon.
- Check honeymoon arrangements.
- Buy going-away outfits, and clothes and luggage for the honeymoon.
- Arrange for wedding clothes to be collected from first-night hotel and stored/returned to hire shops.
- Order currency and/or travellers' cheques for the honeymoon.

- Organize honeymoon transport.
- Make arrangements for pets with neighbours or kennels/cattery.

Two weeks before
- Have hair cut/final practice with hairdresser.
- Have final fitting of wedding dress.
- Hen party.
- Stag party.
- Prepare seating plan.
- Meet photographer and videomaker to finalize arrangements.
- Decide first dance and music and inform DJ/band.
- Decide whether to have a receiving line and advise reception venue.
- Inform reception venue and caterers of the final number of guests.
- Advise florist of the final number of buttonholes and corsages.
- Check bride's father, best man and groom have written their speeches.

One week before
- Make a detailed timetable for your wedding day.
- Hold rehearsal with bride, groom, bride's father, best man, bridesmaids, flower girl, pageboy and ushers.

- Wrap gifts for the wedding party and decide when to give them.
- Check arrangements for flowers, cake, entertainment and transport.
- Decorate wedding cake or arrange to see it at the bakers.
- Advise chief usher of seating plan.
- Father of the bride to check that wedding clothes order is correct and organize collection.
- Do final check on all clothing: try on outfits and wear in wedding shoes.
- Give final confirmation of numbers and any special dietary requirements to reception venue/caterers.
- Do final check on honeymoon plans and any last-minute shopping.
- If you plan to use your car for the wedding and/or honeymoon, check that it's clean and working well.
- Collect foreign currency and travellers' cheques.

One day before
- Make sure best man has a spare set of keys for relevant cars and spare cash.
- Make sure groom has all the messages that need to be read out at the reception.

- Collect any hired clothing and/or accessories.
- Organize delivery of going-away outfit to reception venue/first-night hotel.
- Pack for honeymoon – include clothes, tickets and passports. Have luggage taken to first-night hotel or other convenient location, ready to be picked up the next day.
- Groom to give wedding rings to best man.
- Groom to give fee for the vicar/Registrar/organist to best man.
- If you are organizing the reception catering yourself, do any last-minute defrosting and shopping.
- Deliver cake to the venue and arrange to have it assembled.
- Make sure that the going-away car will be in the right place at the right time.
- Lay out your wedding dress, accessories and jewellery.
- Relax and have an early night.

Take advantage of the Confetti interactive wedding calendar at:
www.confetti.co.uk/weddingplanner/p155

BUDGET PLANNER

This budget planner will help you to manage the cost of your wedding and avoid any nasty surprises! It also tells you who, traditionally, pays for what, although these days there is greater flexibility over financial responsibility. For an interactive budget planner, check out: *www.confetti.co.uk/weddingplanner/p156*

	Who pays	Your estimate £	Actual cost £
WEDDING			
announcements	bride's family		
stationery & postage	bride's family		
church/Registrar's fee	groom		
ceremony/music	bride's family		
transport to ceremony & reception (except for groom & best man)	bride's family		
transport to ceremony for groom & best man	groom/groom's family		
flowers for ceremony & reception	bride's family		
bouquets & buttonholes	groom		
gifts for wedding party	bride/groom		
photographer	bride's family		
videomaker	bride's family		
Total:			
RINGS			
engagement ring	groom		
bride's wedding ring	groom		
groom's wedding ring	bride		
Total:			

	Who pays	Your estimate £	Actual cost £
FASHION & BEAUTY			
wedding dress/outfit	bride's family		
veil/headdress/hat	bride's family		
bride's shoes & accessories	bride's family		
skincare/hairdressing/make-up	bride		
bride's going-away outfit	bride's family		
groom's suit/accessories	groom's family		
bridesmaids' dresses & accessories	bride's family/ bridesmaids		
flower girl's & pageboy's outfits	bride's family		
Total:			
RECEPTION			
hire of venue/ marquee/equipment	bride's family		
wedding cake	bride's family		
entertainment	bride's family		
catering, food & drink	bride's family		
Total:			
HONEYMOON			
first-night accommodation	groom		
travel & accommodation	groom		
spending money	bride & groom		
Total:			
GRAND TOTAL:			

INDEX

Launched in February 1999, confetti.co.uk is the UK's leading wedding web site, helping over 100,000 brides, grooms and guests every month.

Free and easy to use, confetti.co.uk is packed full of ideas and advice to help organize every stage of your wedding. At confetti.co.uk, you can choose from hundreds of beautiful wedding dresses; investigate our list of more than 3,000 wedding and reception venues; plan your wedding; chat to other brides about their experiences; and ask for advice from Aunt Betti, our agony aunt. If your guests are online too, we will even help you set up a wedding web site to share details and photos with your family and friends.

Confetti.co.uk also runs the UK's fastest growing wedding list service, offering unbeatable choice and convenience. To select your gifts you can either go online or order a copy of the confetti.co.uk gift book. Your guests can then order their gifts by phone from one of our wedding consultants or 24 hours a day on the Internet.

If you want your reception to go with a bang, the wedding and party shop at confetti.co.uk stocks everything you need, from stationery to streamers to candles and even disposable cameras. It's ideal for all your special occasions, not only weddings!

To find out more or to order your Confetti gift book or party brochure, visit www.confetti.co.uk, call 0870 840 6060, or e-mail us at info@confetti.co.uk